MEDIA ANTHROPOLOGY

MEDIA ANTHROPOLOGY
INFORMING GLOBAL CITIZENS

Edited by Susan L. Allen

Foreword by Mary Catherine Bateson

BERGIN & GARVEY
Westport, Connecticut • London

Library of Congress Cataloging-in-Publication Data

Media anthropology : informing global citizens / edited by Susan L.
  Allen ; foreword by Mary Catherine Bateson.
     p.   cm.
  Includes bibliographical references and index.
  ISBN 0-89789-342-5 (alk. paper)
    1. Communication in anthropology. 2. Applied anthropology.
  3. Anthropology—Authorship. 4. Motion pictures in ethnology.
  5. Media anthropology.   I. Allen, Susan L.
  GN13.M44   1994
  302.23—dc20   93-17649

British Library Cataloguing in Publication Data is available.

Copyright © 1994 by Susan L. Allen

All rights reserved. No portion of this book may be
reproduced, by any process or technique, without the
express written consent of the publisher.

Library of Congress Catalog Card Number: 93-17649
ISBN: 0-89789-342-5

First published in 1994

Bergin & Garvey, 88 Post Road West, Westport, CT 06881
An imprint of Greenwood Publishing Group, Inc.

Printed in the United States of America

The paper used in this book complies with the
Permanent Paper Standard issued by the National
Information Standards Organization (Z39.48-1984).

10 9 8 7 6 5 4 3 2 1

In tribal societies, people feel kinship with one another and their surroundings, as the "Millennium" television series illustrated so wonderfully for a general audience. Their's is a homogeneous world, but tribal peoples know where they belong and that they have a response/ability for their particular realm of Earth and fellows.

The great challenge facing human beings as we begin a new millennium is to learn to transcend our particular environment and begin to see the whole Earth as our home and its global citizens as our tribe. Like "Millennium," media anthropology, in many forms, can help those who increasingly feel estranged from one another and the environment to re/member our interconnectedness and interdependence. It can do this by sharing the context and perspective we need to move beyond the concrete and exclusive reality of our tribal past and into the larger and, admittedly more diverse and abstract, mutuality that must be our future.

This book is for you "professional strangers" and others who are drawn to participate in this holistic and radically democratic "way of seeing" we are calling media anthropology.

Contents

Acknowledgments	ix
Foreword *Mary Catherine Bateson*	xiii
Introduction *Susan L. Allen*	xvii
1. A Brief History of Media Anthropology *Susan L. Allen*	1
2. What is Media Anthropology? A Personal View and a Suggested Structure *Susan L. Allen*	15
3. The Anthropologist as Magazine Writer *Cynthia Lollar*	33
4. The Anthropologist as Editorial Writer *Randolph Fillmore*	47
5. The Anthropologist as Newspaper Journalist *Thomas Shroder*	61
6. The Anthropologist as Trade Book Author *Jack Weatherford*	67

7.	The Anthropologist as Television Subject *Helen Fisher*	81
8.	The Anthropologist as Television Journalist *James Lett*	91
9.	The Anthropologist as Television Producer *Ira R. Abrams*	105
10.	The Anthropologist as Radio Producer *Ken C. Erickson*	131
11.	The Anthropologist as Media Anthropologist *Susan L. Allen*	145

Postscript: A Cautionary Tale
Susan L. Allen — 161

Bibliography — 165

Index — 169

About the Contributors — 175

Acknowledgments

I want to thank some people who helped shape my brand of media anthropology: the late Conrad C. Reining for his belief in media anthropology and in me; folklorist P. J. Wyatt (who listened in the late 1960s when no one else would); and anthropologists Dorothy K. Billings and the late C.W.M. Hart from Wichita State University (WSU) for teaching me and helping me feel connected with the original anthropology community through their stories about Radcliffe-Brown, Malinowski, and Mead.

I would also like to commend the small WSU anthropology department for providing the "four-field" grounding in anthropology that is the basis of an "anthropological perspective." The critical, comparative thinking skills and generalist's adaptive spirit that can be generated by this unique perspective are critical to the practice of media anthropology and are, I believe, anthropology's great gift to the world.

Thank you to the journalism profession, in general, and communications professor Robert Bontrager, in particular, for showing me the survival value of an informed general public and for teaching me that actually communicating is much different and more important than simply spouting information. Thank you to journalists P. Dell Brinkman, J. Laurence Day, and, especially, intercultural communications scholar Nobleza Asuncion-Landé from the University of Kansas, for enlightening me about the importance of earning one's academic "baseball cap" and for appreciating integration, even in a doctoral program!

Heartfelt *mahalo* to the late, visionary communications scholar Wilbur Schramm and to Jim Richstad, Virginia Cooper Lemon, and Meg White from the East-West Center in Honolulu for helping me get to the very best place on earth to practice media anthropology in 1977.

Thank you to Senator Nancy Landon Kassebaum and Anne S. Butler for hiring a young Ph.D. media anthropologist with the blind faith that surely one of those could provide some useful service.

I want to acknowledge an intellectual debt to some Taoist and tribal sages, Western mystics, and more contemporary rabble-rousers such as Buckminster Fuller, Gregory Bateson, Marshall McLuhan, Clyde Kluckhohn, Alan Watts, Matthew Fox, Carl Rogers, Neil Postman, and Earl Weingartner—and thank them for sharing certain ideas that helped form my own vision of wholeness and participation.

I note with regret that these early idea-models (save one) are males, although of course I knew many inspiring women who were not visible public figures (i.e., were not in the media), my own intellectual, rabble-rouser mother included. I can name many female intellectual models today; however, the absence of women scholars in the media in the 1950s, 1960s, and even 1970s helps explain once again the importance of the late Dr. Margaret Mead to so many of us. Somehow, she forced the powers that be to allow her both to be herself and to be heard.

Beyond the gender issue, I am forever amazed by, and grateful to, Dr. Mead for her intuition that fragmented, exclusive perspectives were incompatible with our times and for having enough confidence in the global citizenry to want to share her energizing inspirations ("Never doubt that a small group of thoughtful, committed citizens can change the world. Indeed, it is the ony thing that ever has.") and her mind-expanding observations (People "can have it not only both ways, but many more than both ways.")—and do it in words we could understand.

Many thanks to the contributors to this book, who allowed me to present their work without benefit of knowing exactly how I

Acknowledgments

was defining "media anthropology." They are not bashful about sharing their own thinking, however, and I know they will be involved in the refinement of the field for many years to come.

Thanks, also to "anthropologist as acquisitions editor" Lynn Flint of Greenwood Publishing Group for her foresight, and to Cathryn Lee, Sasha Kintzler, and Judith Edelstein for their help with the manuscript.

I am deeply grateful to Dr. Mary Catherine Bateson for bringing such wonderful continuity to this project. To paraphrase a think tank from the 1960s (Blood, Sweat and Tears, I think): "Mama may have and papa may have, but God Bless the child who's got her own." Thank you, Dr. Bateson, for providing my (only slightly younger) generation of anthropologists with an appropriately paradoxical model for both "composing our own" and honoring our roots.

My personal thank you to the late George W. Allen, D.V.M., Marge Bernard Allen, Jan Allen, and Deborah S. A. Capalbo for sharing their open-mindedness, curiosity, and optimism. Thank you, finally, to Georgia K. Garrett for her love of mystery and metaphor and for helping me find wholeness in real life.

Foreword

Mary Catherine Bateson

The emergence of a subdiscipline of media anthropology occurs at a time when the place of anthropology in the mass media is of increasing concern to all anthropologists and cannot be left to specialists. Within cultural anthropology, a whole range of new subdisciplines has been defined, including media anthropology. Each of these grows and threatens to divide, like the chapters of this book, into further specializations, and we fear increasing separation. But strange things have been happening to boundaries, opposite trends creating paradoxical conditions. The international borders of nations, for instance, have become more permeable, while at the same time nations, within, are increasingly divided among ethnic enclaves. In anthropology as well, traditional divisions are becoming permeable.

At one time, most anthropologists lived in neatly segmented worlds, each offering considerable privacy: the field, the academy, the home society. In the field the anthropologist was ethnographer—looking, listening and observing, learning the ways of some other community, usually small and exotic. In the academy, the anthropologist was educator and expert. In the society at large, the anthropologist merited mild curiosity and was largely irrelevant. Each sphere of activity called for a different kind of behavior, even a different language.

This is no longer the case. Anthropologists are increasingly acting as liaisons between their research communities and outsiders, while questions of cultural difference have acquired central policy-making importance. Since the 1960s, students have demanded "relevance" or marketability and have judged professors by standards derived from the worlds of entertainment and politics. The emergence of a subdiscipline of anthropologists specializing in communication with the public at large through the modern mass media is a sign not simply of a move by a few anthropologists beyond traditional boundaries but of a restructuring of spheres of activity. Trade books have replaced textbooks and monographs in many classrooms, the Tasaday are headline news, and beginning students have mental images and polemical opinions about the !Kung, the Yanomami, and the Sioux. So do their parents. Increasingly, the !Kung, the Yanomami, and the Sioux know about, and critique, the writings of anthropologists, as ethnography becomes part of the raw material of ethnic identity rather than vice versa. For better or for worse, "culture," in approximately the sense used by anthropologists, is a term that crops up regularly on the daily news.

What this means is that although only a small number of anthropologists will write best-sellers or earn their livings as columnists or talk show hosts, each one of us today lives in a new communicational universe as strange as a new field site, one that feels unsettling and occasionally demeaning.

The discomfort is self-made. It is easy to feel inadequate when familiar ideas become the stuff of debate in such contested areas as "multiculturalism," if anthropologists allow themselves to be slow, inarticulate, and unconsulted. Deep professional commitments to the integrity of cultures and theoretical constructs must now be defended by effective communication that feels embarrassingly like popularization. In fact, clinging to complex technical formulations can itself become a betrayal of the discipline unless these are also recast for accessiblity. Decisions are being made everywhere for which anthropologists have essential input, and it must be made available. The comfortable privacy of the academy is no longer a refuge.

To address the wider society will require new skills, many of which are described in this volume. It will also require changes

Foreword

in the way we deal with each other. Perhaps we could start by setting aside the term *popularization* entirely in speaking of each other's work. Addressing and informing some new group requires skill and analysis. It is the equivalent of functioning within the society as both observer and participant. Mastering a new genre is like learning a new language, acquiring access to a new world. Who better to do this than anthropologists? This does not mean that there is not plenty of bad work done: it appears in professional journals as well as tabloids. This does not mean that the work of anthropologists is not sometimes exploited and distorted by those who use it at second hand: this is why we must learn to do the communicating ourselves.

There are not two audiences, "the profession" and the general public; there are many. Addressing economic development professionals is not the same as addressing grade school children. Health care providers need one kind of cultural knowledge to inform their work, and women adjusting to new cultural possibilities need another. Sermons, stump speeches, and sonnets each have their rules and traditions. Many of the chapters in this volume should be read as first efforts to convey the subcultures of different professional worlds, sometimes phrased in how-to terms. When anthropologists become effective communicators, it is because they pay attention to ethnographies of communication and respect the values of their audiences.

If we can stop speaking scornfully of "popularization," perhaps we can learn to stop snubbing those who earn their living as communicators of anthropological ideas. For all the contention and debate about theory and fashion, anthropologists do share certain basic outlooks, including their respect for cultural difference and their holistic awareness of context. These, as Susan Allen points out, are ideas that anthropologists can and should carry with them wherever they go. It is not necessary to spout jargon in order to maintain professional identities.

A volume such as this suggests yet another kind of change in our internal communications. Simply put, something needs to happen to our professional conversations so that when a phone call comes from a local television station, an academic anthropologist can respond effectively. Workshops at the annual meetings are a start. A skill-oriented volume such as this is also a start. But it is important that we be involved with each other, especially with colleagues on other campuses, in swift and effective discussions of the applications of our knowledge to current issues. What needs to be said *now*? What false assumptions are being made about unfamiliar peoples we have visited? What additional facts are needed for decisions, and who can get them quickly into print? These are basic questions that we need to be able to pose to each other and that parallel the traditional questions of journalism. The American Anthropological Association (AAA) task forces on such matters as hunger or the acquired immunodeficiency syndrome (AIDS) epidemic allow the development of the necessary thinking, but so far they have depended on rather slow and formal means of communication. A more effective method would be the development of topical computer conferencing within the profession. Every kind of communication has its characteristic way of handling time and space. Effective interaction with the broadcast media requires the skills of abolishing space and accelerating time.

This volume proposes new skills and new attitudes. It suggests a level of awareness and respect that should become part of the background of everyone in the profession. New structures and new kinds of literacy are also needed to support the habits of topicality. At a time when more and more decisions require the contributions of anthropologists, no small group of virtuosos or specialists can be sufficient for the task.

Introduction

Susan L. Allen

When you are on a mountain, you cannot see its true shape.
—Chinese proverb

In his book *The Turning Point*, physicist and social commentator Fritjof Capra said: In the future, journalists "will change their thinking from fragmentary to holistic modes and develop a new professional ethic based on social and ecological awareness. Instead of concentrating on sensational presentations of aberrant, violent, and destructive happenings, reporters and editors will have to analyze the complex social and cultural patterns that form the context of such events" (Capra 1982, 409).

"We need a new journalism," says international development scholar John Galtung (1984, 1). We need "a global journalism, liberating from visible and invisible repression, capable of reflecting in its social communication the global nature of our problems" (1984), 1). Galtung argued that only if journalists "break out of their thought prisons" can this new type of journalism emerge.

At the same time that journalism is finding itself at a loss how to help people acquire the context and perspectives they need to survive in our complex environment, professional anthropology

—whose purpose is to build a whole-world cognitive database and show how the details of life interact so we can develop an "anthropological" or "holistic" perspective—has matured as a science, and anthropologists are feeling pressure to let go of their exotic, remote concentration and participate in what is fretfully known to those in academe as "the real world."

It is into this setting media anthropology emerges to suggest first, that the criticisms of today's crisis-oriented journalism are accurate due largely to the media's use of a reactionary and reductionistic reporting style that focuses on the immediate and the particular while ignoring the "big picture." Second, that the perspectives available from anthropology can help journalism "add a W for the whole" to its traditional "who, what, when, where, why" reporting structure (see chapter 11) as a way more adequately to inform global citizens in the twenty-first century. That is, anthropology can help build holistic perspectives to the degree that anthropologists can get beyond our own fragmented (and increasingly particularistic) perceptions of the world and of our role in public discourse about it. It is important to recall that we anthropologists learned about the world from limited perspectives like everyone else on the planet; the notion of whole-Earth considerations is new to all of us except, perhaps, the poets and mystics. In fact, the name anthropology itself reflects a more hierarchal, male-centered (andropocentric), and human-centered (anthropocentric) worldview than the inclusive, ecological one we are evolving today.

But anthropology is unique among all of Western science in its potential to build contextual frameworks on which to hang the scattered details of life and evoke a perspective that asks us to see the seemingly separate aspects of life in that context, as part of their larger whole. Through some inspired vision or magical piece of synchronicity, the theories and methods that can provide a framework for global, intercultural, and perhaps even holistic perspectives were developed by the profession of anthropology as it generated the tools to understand "whole" cultures. It is now up to us anthropologists to learn to apply these methods and theories—and the perspectives they make possible—to issues of the day, within a global context.

For example, as American Anthropological Association past-president Annette B. Weiner and anthropologist Mary Catherine

Introduction xix

Bateson recently asked in a *Chronicle of Higher Education* article (1992), "Where are the anthropologists?" in the current, befuddled national debate on multiculturalism! The absence of an anthropological voice in this debate is being sorely felt—as it is in most other topical issues. I suggest this is primarily because what we need to aid understanding of these complex topics is not "more information" but some context and perspective for the information we have.

It seemed perfectly reasonable and natural to me, as a 20-year-old studying anthropology in the late 1960s, to think anthropologists could appear on the "Dick Cavett" and "Johnny Carson" shows or write for magazines. Margaret Mead was doing it all the time. There she was calming us down, cheerfully providing a pattern or comparison that helped make sense of some of the commotion in our lives. Do today's anthropologists realize what a powerful "perspective-building" tool their discipline can evoke or what their unique professional training can bring to journalism and, consequently, to public perceptions?

Marvin Harris (1991) noted that of all academic disciplines, anthropology is unique in the kind of global coverage and comparative perspective that this book is suggesting could help alleviate what has become a serious public education/citizen participation problem.

Other people-centered disciplines tend to study only a particular segment of human experience or a particular time or place of our cultural or biological development, Harris said. "The distinction of anthropology is that it is global and comparative" (Harris 1991, 4).

"Anthropologists insist first and foremost that conclusions based upon the study of one particular human group or civilization be checked against the evidence of other groups or civilizations." In this way, he said, "anthropologists hope to transcend the biases of their own sex, class, tribe, race, nation, religion, or culture" (1991, 5). He also said that "in anthropological perspective," all people and cultures are equally worthy of our attention.

> Anthropology is incompatible with the view of those who would have themselves and no one else represent humanity, stand at the pinnacle of progress, or be chosen by God or history to fashion the world in their own image. By adopting this broad view of the

totality of human experience perhaps we humans can tear off the blinders put on us by our local life-style and see ourselves as we really are. (1991, 5)

Like perfect truth, a truly holistic perspective is, of course, impossible to attain. It would be a "God's-eye" view. However, sensitivity to the concept itself can tune us in (via our information bearers) to the enormous system of adaptive alternatives that supersede any fragmented view. Just that seemingly small "switch in our visual gestalt," as someone previously has tagged such a profound perception change, will make us wiser world citizens and more capable stewards of our interconnected environment.

However, if information and insights that can help "tear off the blinders" are to reach the great multitude of global citizens, the media will bring them to us. More than ever before, anthropologists, like all educators, need to begin meeting people "where they live," both linguistically and logistically. Simply put, this will mean communicating through readily available media and in widely acceptable styles and formats.

MEDIA ANTHROPOLOGY

Media anthropology is a proposed new subdiscipline for both anthropology and the communications professions that synthesizes aspects of journalism and anthropology for the explicit purpose of sensitizing as many of Earth's citizens as possible to anthropological or holistic perspectives.

If professionals trained in a combination of perspective-building methods and media communication do not bring us our news and information, then who will, and what will be their training? Who will create our image of the world and share, or not share, the tools to participate in it?

Someone is going to do the reporting; someone is going to do the educating; and some manner of cultural, global, and universal perspective will be disseminated. We who are dependent on the mass media for our view of the world and of ourselves have the right to demand thoughtful selection and presentation of the information that will set our agendas and our boundaries. We

Introduction   xxi

anthropologists and journalists and we who will be media anthropologists have the responsibility—and the opportunity—to help provide this information (Allen 1984).

THE MEDIA ANTHROPOLOGISTS

There have long been individual anthropologists who have "used the media" to "tell us about the world," some with greater success and accuracy than others. What "media anthropologists" bring to the considerable efforts of our predecessors is a deliberate and systematic intent to bring perspective-building information and insights to media audiences in the regular course of our jobs, in some cases, along with professional careers in academic anthropology and, in some cases, through positions within the media themselves.

We practice media anthropology in a variety of ways and subscribe to no one definition of it. As no formal training in media anthropology yet exists within an integrated academic degree program, contributors to this volume came to this "praxis" of theory and action individually and will help refine the definition of the field as the discipline unfolds. A commitment to sharing anthropologically oriented information and insights "beyond academe" is the common goal that led them to media anthropology. All have worked successfully in the particular medium about which they write.

IN THIS BOOK

We begin this first book about media anthropology with a look at its brief history. In chapter 2, I open professional and public discussion on the parameters of media anthropology by offering a personal view of its meaning and its raison d'être. On subsequent pages, eight professional anthropologists/journalists/filmmakers/authors/professors/communications officers/museum researchers (i.e., media anthropologists) tell their sometimes humorous and always practical tales of "doing" media anthropology with an eye to how readers may follow suit.

With the exception of Helen Fisher, who is a physical anthropologist, I want to note that contributors to this book come mostly from social/cultural anthropology. We are well aware, however, of contributions being made to an informed public by anthropologists from wider backgrounds. In fact I join the many others who are distressed at a threatened "fission" of the American-style, four-field integrative model of anthropology, which I believe generates the foundation upon which anthropology's—and media anthropology's—holistic perspective rests (Brown and Yoffee 1992).

I also want to add that, although we are Americans talking about a global information phenomenon, in the spirit of "think globally, act locally," we wanted to begin somewhere.

Most readers are familiar with contributors Ira Abrams, Helen Fisher, and Jack Weatherford, an Emmy Award winner and two best-selling authors, respectively. But the rest of us (some of whom are well known among local media audiences) are living examples of our strong belief that many anthropologists, trained and motivated, can practice media anthropology.

Our purpose is to introduce the concept of media anthropology—in a straightforward, how-we-do-it format—to anthropologists who may want to begin working in the media and to journalists who want some insight into the kind of contextual background that anthropology can bring to topical media material. We hope this collection will help initiate the creation of an academic degree program in media anthropology to train students from backgrounds in both anthropology and the various communications disciplines who would like to pursue this important new form of public education in the future.

REFERENCES

Allen, Susan. 1984. "Media Anthropology: Building Public Perspective." *Anthropology Newsletter* 25, no. 8: 6.

———. 1991. "Adding a W: How Journalists Can Practice Media Anthropology." *Journalism Educator* 42, no. 2: 21-23.

Brown, Peter J., and Norman Yoffee. 1992. "Is Fission the Future of Anthropology?" (Special Report). *Ideas in Anthropology.* Santa Fe, NM: School of American Research.

Capra, Fritjof. 1982. *The Turning Point.* New York: Simon and Schuster.

Coughlin, Ellen K. 1992. "Anthropologists Ask How They Wound Up in

the Wings of Multiculturalism," *Chronicle of Higher Education* 34: A8.
Galtung, John. 1984. "A New Order Is Not Enough," *Media Development*. (April 1984): 1.
Harris, Marvin. 1987. *Cultural Anthropology*, 3d ed. New York: HarperCollins Publishing, Inc.

MEDIA ANTHROPOLOGY

Chapter 1

A Brief History of Media Anthropology

Susan L. Allen

> Isolated from the public by university walls, glass exhibit cases and jargon which makes his language difficult to comprehend, the anthropologist and his fellow academicians have neglected to communicate with the general public. This lack . . . is being seriously felt.
>
> —*Media Anthropologist Newsletter* 1, no. 1, 1972

Some observers believe that media anthropology has existed since the beginnings of anthropology; they are correct if we focus on the isolated and occasional writings and productions of a few early and contemporary anthropologists who have been willing to communicate beyond academe. The other extreme position, that media anthropology still exists mostly within the imagination of a few adherents, also has its proponents.

If social psychologist Gordon W. Allport's observation is correct—that most people do not become converts in advance; they are converted by the *faits accomplis*—my view is that the future of media anthropology is about to begin.

Although a few famous anthropologists and many non-anthropologist communicators have disseminated anthropologically oriented information through media channels since the media were invented, professional anthropologists can reasonably mark the beginning of a conscious movement to organize a subdiscipline and profession of media anthropology at just under 25 years ago, following the 1969 meetings of the American Anthropological Association (AAA). Like other important social change movements from that era, the search by anthropologists (and serious communicators, as well) for ways to reach citizens with information and insights that could sensitize them to the newly realized global environment began in many places almost at once. But, also like other change movements, it has been a grassroots effort that traditionalists are only now beginning to take seriously.

The term *media anthropology* itself was coined in the brief flurry of activity following the 1969 AAA meetings. The absence of information from the scientists to the public concerning the infamous Jensen Report on race and IQ, presented at the meeting—and the misinformation that did enter media channels—crystallized the concern of a growing number of anthropologists about both the dearth of public knowledge of anthropological concepts and their own lack of skills and channels to disseminate them. Recognition of the seriousness of this communications barrier, as well as a concern among some anthropologists that they "were not doing all they could do to further social change and advancement in the U.S.A." (Topper 1976, 25), led to an investigation of the feasibility of what anthropologists decided to call media anthropology.

FIRST MEDIA ANTHROPOLOGY GATHERING

An AAA Media Workshop followed the 1969 meeting, during the summer of 1970. A small cadre of anthropologists, under the leadership of the late Conrad C. Reining, then chair of the Department of Anthropology at Catholic University, undertook the novel study of the relationship of anthropology and the media. They met with reporters, producers, and science writers who were engaged professionally with the communication of science information and who shared the anthropologist's desire to get more of that information to the public.

Participants at the Media Workshop included such prominent journalist/communicators as the science editor of the *Washington*

Post, the assistant chief of the National Geographic Society News Service, the science information officer of the Smithsonian Institution, and the Washington editor of *Psychology Today*, as well as representatives from other professional and governmental organizations such as the National Institute of Mental Health (NIMH) and the National Science Foundation (NSF).

Workshop topics included media attitudes toward anthropology and science in general, the anthropologist's attitudes toward the media (which may be summed up as mutual avoidance), views of the American public concerning anthropological and other scientific subject matter, and the media techniques that anthropologists might use. The workshop ended by making four specific recommendations, modest by today's media-conscious standards, but two of them produced some immediate results. The workshop recommended:

1. A public information office for the AAA to function as a liaison between the press and professional anthropologists.
2. A newsroom for the national meetings of the AAA.
3. A glossary to translate jargon into vocabulary easily understood.
4. A regular, syndicated newspaper column related to anthropology.

SOME RESULTS

Encouraged by the readership of Margaret Mead's *Redbook* magazine column, I took the first step toward creating an anthropologically oriented newspaper column. Reining informed me in 1972 that I, unknowingly, had begun a research project specifically focusing on one of the four workshop recommendations. An article, "Predicting Reader Interest in Anthropology Column," prepared from the subsequent master's thesis, appeared in *Journalism Quarterly* (Allen 1975) and proved encouraging to the new media anthropologists. It showed that in fact the general citizenry would accept a regular dose of anthropologically oriented information, if it were thoughtfully presented, and that the media (newspapers, in this case) could provide workable channels for presenting it.

The second workshop recommendation to receive immediate attention was the one proposing a newsroom for future AAA meetings. A newsroom was established at the following national meeting, and from it the AAA released its first press release in 70 years! (A third recommendation did not see results until 1989, when a Public Information Office was established by the AAA.)

In addition to these early events, a newsletter called *Media Anthropologist* was started by Reining and two other workshop participants, anthropologists Martin Topper and Charlene James. Its purpose was to try to build a bridge between anthropologists and the media by establishing regular communications. It was published from 1972 to 1974 and had a circulation of nearly 500. Reining said in a 1978 letter that both he and James, the editor, thought the newsletter's function was viable and that it could be revived. It would take another 12 years, however, before a similar newsletter, *Anthro-Journalism*, appeared through the auspices of the new Washington, D.C.,-based Center for Anthropology and Journalism.

Interest in media anthropology proved enduring among a slowly growing number of public education-oriented anthropologists, however. Besides those few famous anthropologists who had used the media for many years, Topper and E. B. Eiselein presented the work of several anthropologists in a special symposium issue of the Society for Applied Anthropology journal, *Human Organization*, on "Media Anthropology" in 1976. By 1977, Eiselein and Topper had collected a "Directory of Media Anthropologists," which identified 44 anthropologists who were working with the media in limited ways, and we now know there were more evolving media anthropologists around the globe. However, media anthropology was such a new concentration at the time that few jobs existed and no significant support was forthcoming from traditional anthropology, traditional journalism, or funding agencies for two noteworthy historical reasons.

First, as Mary Catherine Bateson points out in the Foreword to this book, the anthropology community has never supported efforts by professional anthropologists to communicate with the public because it believed that "popularization" sacrifices academic credibility. In fact, some "popular accounts" of "exotic

A Brief History

natives" have respected neither the subject matter nor the audience, as we well know. (The argument of media anthropology, however, is that silencing anthropologists is not the way to improve such negligence; rather, inaccurate and/or ineffective public information can be better addressed by training media anthropologists.)

Second, on the other side of the media anthropology coin, publishers and broadcasters continued their claim well into the late 1980s that their audiences had "no interest" in anthropologically oriented information, so why hire anyone trained to provide it? In fact, producing stories that could expose audiences to holistic and intercultural perspectives was, in the past, commonly referred to among journalists as "Afghanistanism" (meaning "no one knows or cares about it"), and because of this history of avoidance by anthropologists and journalists, that claim became at least partially accurate.

How can the public express interest in something we know nothing about? Journalism does not tell us what to think, but, as someone once quipped, it does guide what we "think about." When the Soviets invaded the actual country of Afghanistan, hardly anyone beyond a small circle of specialists even knew where it was on a map, let alone how conflict and oppression in faraway places can impact our own lives. For that matter, few of us knew anything about the former Soviet Union either, beyond crisis-oriented hyperbole. This information vacuum still exists today.

Those impediments aside, a small number of anthropologists and others (working independently and without benefit of knowing their scattered colleagues or uniting goals) continued making progress toward creating this new field designed to help alleviate the problems caused by journalism's fragmented, one-dimensional information and anthropology's inability and unwillingness to apply its methods and perspectives to current events and communicate with the public. These anthropologists worked in an imaginative variety of ways.

For example, Reining's interest in practicing anthropology beyond academe led him to help establish the Washington Association for Practicing Anthropologists and teach the first media anthropology course at Catholic University. James went to work for the Smithsonian Institution, where she became manager of the public education–focused Seminar and Lecture Program. Eiselein organized media-literacy workshops for professional anthropologists and produced anthropologically oriented programs for KUAT-TV and AM in Arizona while developing a media research agency. Topper began working in the Southwest as a psychotherapist and medical administrator for the Indian Health Service while consulting for media projects. (See also Eiselein and Topper 1976.)

Because I was only beginning my doctoral studies at that time, I had the opportunity to guide an academic program with the goal of formulating a new subdiscipline that went beyond anthropologists' "using" the media to actually synthesizing the training and practice of both anthropology and journalism, including communications studies, in general. To illustrate the assorted positions one media anthropological career can encompass, I will add that my own work has so far included conducting research on international news flow in the Pacific Islands, editing an international journal for communicators, publishing a small multiethnic newspaper in Kansas, writing on social issues for a U.S. senator, working as a visiting researcher at an institute for multimedia education in Japan, writing a model media anthropology newspaper column, working on the staff of a university mental health facility; and those were the "good jobs"! I share this list to point out the need for people in new fields of endeavor to "create their own jobs" rather than to boast of a contest among organizations to hire media anthropologists! However, it is a monumental understatement to say there is plenty of work to do; and, that in diverse positions, it is possible to do one's work as a media anthropologist, bringing holistic and intercultural perspectives to bear on the particular subject matter involved. Most other early media anthropologists also went to work creating media products with a resolve to retain the academic integrity of the material while reinvigorating it for a general audience.

I present a chronology of the movement to create a subdiscipline of media anthropology from 1969 to 1993. This list does not include all early or even all contemporary anthropologists who have used the media as a tool to disseminate their works. Rather, it concentrates on developments directly relevant to the creation of organized media anthropology.

A Brief History

Before beginning this look at the current media anthropology movement, however, I want to stress the fact that—although communication by anthropologists through media channels has always been a rare and individual occurrence—media anthropology did not appear out of thin air in 1969. We honor a long line of anthropologists who came before us, beginning with the designated founder of American anthropology, Franz Boas, who demonstrated his own understanding of the need for an informed general citizenry, notably through the inspiration of his many media-oriented students: Margaret Mead, Edward Sapir, novelist Zora Neale Hurston, and W.E.B. DuBois, to name a few. (See Bishop 1985 for more on anthropology and the press.)

Readers undoubtedly will be able to add their own influences and media mentors from the small, but active, group of "science writers" who have appeared in the media through the years and who (consequently) probably introduced them to anthropology—some from anthropology and some from biology and other sciences: Loren Eisley, Edward T. Hall, Marshall McLuhan, Joseph Campbell, Jane Goodall, Walter Goldschmidt, the Leakey family, Stephen J. Gould, Laura Bohannon (a.k.a. Elenore Smith Bowen), David Maybury-Lewis, and more, including several contributors to this book, and I would like to add Bill Moyers, Tom Wolfe, V. S. Naipaul, and some of the other culturally sensitive journalists and trade book authors.

We stand on the shoulders of these media-oriented anthropologists and other scientists and recognize that media anthropology owes much to their efforts.

The challenge of media anthropology is to join this group. To paraphrase media anthropologist Martin Topper, 100 media stories by or about the work of one "superstar" anthropologist are helpful but, in the long run, 100 stories by 100 media anthropologists are a more efficient way to bring anthropological perspectives to the public. The remainder of this book addresses this latter, more systematic and democratic form of media anthropology.

Some citations in the following list illustrate samples of successful media anthropological products, and some represent important events. It is a "working" list, and, although it looks here like a large number of people and products, these anthropologist/communicators and their works still represent rare exceptions to the continuing rule of ardent mutual avoidance between anthropologists and the media.

A Working Chronology of Media Anthropology from 1969 to 1993

Pre-1969	Popular works by Margaret Mead, Ruth Benedict, Gregory Bateson, Ashley Montagu, Clyde Kluckhohn, Hortense Powdermaker, Laura Bohannon, Lionel Tiger, Alan Lomax, Marvin Harris, Colin Turnbull, Walter Goldschmidt, Edward T. Hall, other anthropologists (mostly in book form)
1969	American Anthropological Association meeting in New Orleans that led to seminal Media Workshop
1970	AAA Summer Media Workshop, organized by Conrad C. Reining and funded by the Wener-Gren Foundation
1970	Newsroom established at San Diego AAA meetings (issued first press release in 70 years)
1970s	Mass Media Internships for anthropologists sponsored by the Russell Sage Foundation; occasional workshops on media and science sponsored by the AAA, American Association for the Advancement of Science (AAAS), NSF, the National Association of Editors and Broadcasters (NAEB), Russell Sage, and other organizations
1970s	E. B. Eiselein employed as a media anthropologist by KUAT-TV and AM in Arizona
1972-1974	*Media Anthropologist* newsletter established at Prince George Community College, edited by Charlene James (with assistance from Conrad Reining and Martin Topper)
1972	First Media Anthropology university course, taught by Conrad Reining at Catholic University
1972	Media anthropology radio and television work by Martin Topper at Southern Methodist University
1973	Demonstration pressroom at several AAA division meetings
1975	"Predicting Reader Interest in Anthropology Column," Susan L. Allen, *Journalism Quarterly*, spring issue
1976	"Media Anthropology," a special symposium issue of *Human Organization*, E. B. Eiselein and Martin Topper, eds., June
1976	University of Southern California Center for Visual Anthropology founded by Ira R. Abrams (related to media anthropology)

A Brief History 9

1977	"Directory of Media Anthropologists," compiled by E. B. Eiselein and Martin Topper (listing forty-four anthropologists working with the media)
1977	Committee on External Relations of the AAA Executive Board promotes development of "Outreach Anthropology" to expose wider audiences to anthropology
1978	Series of columns on popular topics in anthropology, *Grand Rapids Sunday Magazine*, by Molly Schuchat, representing the media work of many anthropologists scattered around the globe
1980	First Ph.D. in Media Anthropology, Susan L. Allen (*Media Anthropology: Concept and Pacific Islands Case Study*, Special Studies Program, University of Kansas)
1980s	Mass market media work by William Beeman for the Pacific News Service (column); Maria Vesperi for the *St. Petersburg Times*; other works by Deborah Tannen, Mary Catherine Bateson, Marvin Harris, Mel Konner, Katherine Verdery, and more, including contributors to this book
1982	*The Sex Contract*, Helen E. Fisher, became alternate selection for the Book-of-the-Month Club
1982	Margaret Mead Award established by the AAA and the Society for Applied Anthropology, "for interpretation of anthropological data and principles for the general public." (Mary Lindsay Elmendory, 1982; Ruthann Knudson, 1983; Sue E. Estroff, 1984; Susan Scrimshaw, 1985; Jill E. Korbin, 1986; Myra Bluebond-Langer, 1987; Alex Stepick, 1988; Mark Nichter, 1989; Wenda Trevathan, 1990; Will Roscoe, 1991; Leo R. Chavez, 1992)
1983	National Association for the Practice of Anthropology (NAPA) founded (related to media anthropology)
1983	First M.A. degree in Media Anthropology, Dave Kendall (Special Studies Program, University of Kansas)
1984	"Faces of Culture" series, produced by Ira R. Abrams, wins an Emmy Award
1984	"Expanding the Public Interest: Popular Anthropology Is Perhaps More Popular Than Ever," profile of anthropologist Helen E. Fisher, and "Media Anthropology: Building a Public Perspective," Susan L. Allen, *Anthropology Newsletter*, November issue
1985	"Text and Context in Ethnography and Journalism: A Com-

	parison," session at AAA meetings. Participants included Maria Vesperi, Jane Kramer, James Lett, Bruce Grindal, Willian Robin Ridington, Richard Eder, Erve Chambers, and Vincent Crapanzano
1985	"More on Media Anthropology," James Lett, *Anthropology Newsletter* 26, March 1985
1985	"The Worldview and Ethos of Television Journalism," James Lett paper presented at AAA national meetings
1985	Council for the Advancement and Support of Education (CASE) award to model media anthropology newspaper column, Susan L. Allen
1986	"Anthropology and the Public: Communicating to a Wider Audience," session at AAA meetings. Participants included Helen Fisher, Ruth Oselig, John E. Pfeiffer, Ira R. Abrams, Marilyn Salvador, Ralph J. Bishop, William O. Beeman, Marvin Harris, Barbara Pillsbury
1986	"Extending Ethnography with Visual Anthropology," a paper by John Collier at the Visual Anthropology–sponsored session, AAA national meetings
1986	"Anthropology and Journalism," James Lett, *Communicator*, May issue
1987	Center for Anthro-Journalism (now Center for Anthropology and Journalism) established by Randolph Fillmore
1987	"Anthropological Methods Relevant for Journalists," S. Elizabeth Bird, and "Journalism and Anthropology Share Several Similarities," Bruce T. Grindall and Robin Rhodes, *Journalism Educator*, winter issue
1987	"Adding a W: How Journalists Can Practice Media Anthropology," Susan L. Allen, *Journalism Educator*, summer issue
1987	"An Anthropological View of Television Journalism," James Lett, *Human Organization* 46, 1987
1987	"An Anthropologist at the Anchor Desk," James Lett, *Practicing Anthropologists* 9
1987	"When Religion Makes the Headlines: Journalism as Ethnography in Mexico," a paper by Barbara Jo Lantz, AAA national meetings
1988	"Media Watch" (later "Media Monitor") column established by editor David B. Givens in *Anthropology Newsletter*
1988	Society for Media Anthropology organizational session,

A Brief History

	AAA meetings (Board Members: Randolph Fillmore, James Lett, Susan Allen, Helen Fisher, Maria Vesperi, Bruce Grindall, Molly Schuchat, Cynthia Lollar)
1989	AAA press officer position established, Randolph Fillmore named
1989	*Indian Givers*, Jack Weatherford, selected for Quality Paperback Book-of-the-Month Club
1989	"Training in Media Anthropology," Susan L. Allen, Visual Anthropology column, *Anthropology Newsletter*, May issue
1989	*Anthro-Journalism*, newsletter of the Center for Anthro-Journalism (Center for Journalism and Anthropology) established in October
1989	"Media Anthropology Past, Present and Future," first formal meeting of the proposed Society for Media Anthropology, AAA national meetings, sponsored by NAPA. Participants included Randolph Fillmore, Helen Fisher, E. B. Eiselein, Jean Susan Forward, James Lett, Susan L. Allen
1989	"Performing Journalism: Going Native as Applied Anthropology," Mark Peterson, representing many media/anthropology papers presented at the Center for Anthro-Journalism, Washington, D.C.
1989	"How to Deal with the News Media," James Lett, in *World Class Service*
1989	Establishment of a Committee for Media Anthropology within the General Anthropology Division of the AAA, Molly Schuchat, chair; Helen Fisher, chair-elect
1989	Center for Anthropology and Journalism Award for Excellence established. Recipients: Ron Martz, 1989; Jack Weatherford, 1990; John Nobel Wilford, 1991; Michael Dorris, 1992
1990s	New popular books by several anthropologists, including Jack Weatherford (*Native Roots*), Helen Fisher (*Anatomy of Love*), Mary Catherine Bateson (*Composing a Life*), Deborah Tannen (*You Just Don't Understand*)
1990	AAA national meeting media-related sessions: "Mass Mediations." Participants included Catherine Lutz, Elizabeth Traube, Lila Abu-Lughod, Marilyn Ivy, Jane Collins, Arjun Apadura "The Ethnographic Realities of Mass Communication." Participants included Elizabeth P. Hahn, John L. Caughey,

	Andrew P. Painter, Richard Wilk, Gary Granzberg, Susan Rodgers, Conrad Kottak. (This session provided a good example of "research media anthropology.")
	"Anthropology, Ethics and the Media." Participants included William O. Beeman, Helen Fisher, Mark A. Peterson, Kenneth Newman, Alexandra Close, Mary Catherine Bateson
1991	Year-long "Going Public" series in *Anthropology Newsletter*
1991	Widely popular "Millennium" PBS series by David Maybury-Lewis
1991	Anthropology News Network (ANN) established at the newly relocated Center for Anthropology and Journalism, University of South Florida, Tampa
1991	"Television and the Mediation of Culture: Issues in British Ethnographic Film" session at the AAA national meetings. Participants included Annette B. Weiner, Faye D. Ginsburg, Terence Turner, Leslie Woodhead, Melissa Llewelyn-Davies, Andre Singer, David Turton, Jay Ruby
1992	Society for Applied Anthropology ad hoc committee on media relations organized by J. A. Paredes
1992	"Culture and Mass Media: Production and Reception" session at AAA meetings. Participants included Tamar Gordon, Mayfair Mei-Hui Yang, Nancy Sullivan, Caroline S. Tauxe, Frances E. Mascia-Lees, Patricia Sharpe, Barry D. Dornfeld
1992	Papers at the national AAA meetings on media aspects of the Thomas-Hill hearings by Velma L. Ward and Diann McMahon Dincolo
1993	*ANN Focus*, vol. 1, no. 1, a news and information magazine from the Anthropology News Network

As this chronology illustrates, by 1980 media activity by anthropologists had increased to the point that those individuals interested in the praxis of anthropology and the communications media began to discover one another, to see the common threads now defined as media anthropology running through their varied work, and to organize.

By the late 1980s, a newer group of anthropologists, many of whom had worked in the media and assumed a greater media

A Brief History

orientation in the world (and therefore their work), once again ignited the movement toward creation of a new subdiscipline and profession of media anthropology.

The growing number of media-related sessions at the AAA national meetings illustrates the small, but important, public education thrust that has begun within the traditional anthropology community. In fact, of six anthropologists honored for their contributions to the field at the 1992 AAA meetings, four awards were communications-related: Charles Leslie and Douglas W. Schwartz "for contributions to the increase and dissemination of anthropological knowledge"; and Jack Weatherford and Jean Rouch for "communication of anthropology to the general public." By 1993, world events seem finally to have convinced almost everyone that global, intercultural perspectives are necessary and that anthropology can join forces with the communications professions to help bring them to the general citizenry.

The fall 1992 issue of *Practicing Anthropology* included a commentary on "making use of the media" and provided us with even more names to add to a constantly growing list of anthropologists now tentatively speaking out through media channels: Linda Lenz, Fred Hess, Joanna Brown, Lorna McDougall, Karen Curtis, and more. Author Ann Jordan wrote that NAPA is planning to "continue exploring the ways in which we can communicate anthropological insights to a variety of audiences." She wrote:

> Working with the media involves skills few of us learned in our graduate programs, yet it is becoming a significant and even crucial area for many of us in our work. Furthermore, working with the media is essential if anthropology is to be recognized as a field with relevant and applicable expert knowledge. Terms such as "global economy," "multicultural education," and "managing diversity" have become buzz words which we hear daily in the news and in our offices. Typically the cast of experts discussing the topic does not include an anthropologist. The public in general and frequently our colleagues in related fields are unaware that anthropology is a discipline of the 1990s with specialists at work in a wide variety of applied and public policy areas. We have a responsibility to the future health of our discipline and to the future health of our society to publicize our expertise in these areas. (Jordan 1992)

REFERENCES

Allen, Susan L. 1975. "Predicting Reader Interest in Anthropology Column." *Journalism Quarterly* 52 (Spring): 124-128.
_____. 1980. "Media Anthropology: Concept and Pacific Islands Case Study." Ph.D. diss., University of Kansas, Lawrence.
_____. 1989. "Training in Media Anthropology." *Anthropology Newsletter* 30 (May): 15.
Bishop, Ralph. 1985. "Stones, Bones, and Margaret Mead: The Image of American Anthropology in the General Press, 1927-1983," *Anthropology Newsletter* 26 (April): 18-19.
Eiselein, E. B., and Martin Topper. 1976. "Media Anthropology." *Human Organization* 35 (June): 111-220.
Jordan, Ann. 1992. "Commentary: Making Use of the Media." *Practicing Anthropology* 14, no. 4, Fall: 2.
Topper, Martin D. 1976. "Anthropology and the Mass Media or 'Why Is There A Margaret Mead, Daddy?'" *Council for Anthropology and Education Quarterly* (February): 25-28.

Chapter 2

What is Media Anthropology? A Personal View and a Suggested Structure

Susan L. Allen

Our greatest challenge is to make the world safe for differences.
—John F. Kennedy

MEDIA ANTHROPOLOGY: A PERSONAL VIEW

Media anthropology is amorphous by nature, but its aim is simple and straightforward: in its applied form, media anthropology synthesizes some of the theories, methods, channels, training, and purposes of anthropology and journalism/mass communications for the purpose of sharing "anthropological" perspectives with media audiences; and in its research form, media anthropology studies the communications process from anthropological perspectives. No matter what form the media anthropological communications may take—news story, novel, radio script, cartoon, television appearance, research report—or what the particular subject matter of the piece may be, the underlying aim of media anthropology is to bring the integrative, holistic perspective of anthropology to media information and share it with the general public.

Although this integrative aim is relatively clear-cut, it continues to baffle some people because it also requires a change in attitude. We are so accustomed to viewing our world from narrow, guided perspectives that, as "media astronomer" Carl Sagan says of space, concepts asking us to think about the world as an integrated whole seem "Big. Really Big." Many people refuse to make the effort.

Journalist and satirist Calvin Trillin reflected the thinking of most journalists when he said: "I've decided to skip 'holistic.' I don't know what it means, and I don't want to know. That may seem extreme, but I followed the same strategy toward 'Gestalt' and the Twist, and lived to tell the tale" (Winokur 1987, 137).

The problem this attitude creates for the rest of us is ignoring that we live in an interconnected and interdependent world is becoming increasingly dangerous and foolhardy. Dismissing perspective-building concepts that will give us insights about the world and our lives is like dismissing satellite photographs when predicting the weather or ignoring the disease theory while diagnosing illness. Holism and perspective are important tools that allow us to extricate ourselves from the details of life so we can begin to see that all seemingly separate "parts" of it belong to one integrated system. They also challenge us to overcome the exclusive, crisis-oriented, "soap opera" worldview that many people have found such a comfortable state of mind for so long.

An interesting way to visualize the "reductionist" reporting style that leads to narrow perspectives was created by Karl Popper from the University of London (Smith 1976) to show how our entire Western scientific worldview sets boundaries that preclude connection-making, holistic perspectives.

In Figure 2.1, the searchlights represent our scientific worldview; the airplanes represent seemingly isolated sets of data that science discovers and names reality; and the arch illustrates the actual universe of possibilities.

Popper was suggesting that science defines reality from the perspective established by its "tools." I am borrowing the metaphor to suggest that journalism, with its tools, places parallel limits on our information and, thus, our worldview. The point is that *any* single point of view (searchlight) is too limiting. The tools of science, of journalism, of any one culture, any one religion, and so on are of limited utility when viewing life as an integrated whole. The worldview of any group and generation

What is Media Anthropology?

Figure 2.1
How Science and Journalism Reduce Our Worldview

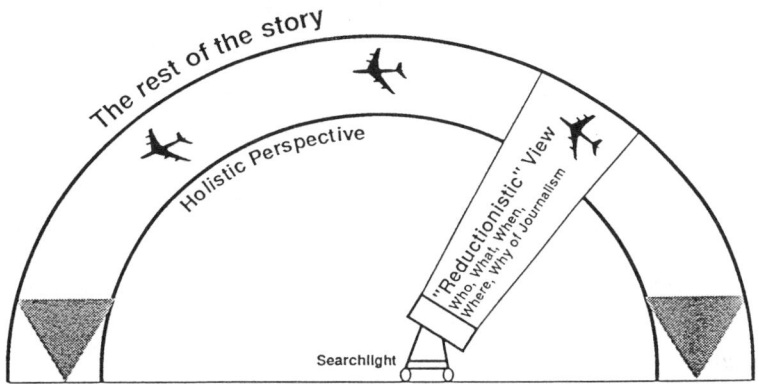

can never be understood apart from the conditioning environment in which it is formulated. All "ways of seeing" are partial.

Like the view from a house with only one window, we are all born believing there is only one available perspective on the world: our own. However, to extend the house analogy, we actually live in something more like an old three-story home with lots and lots of windows, but the shades are drawn on all of the windows except one. We are born looking out of this one window. The direction of our worldview is provided by the particular circumstances of our own genes and experiences and the agreed-upon beliefs of our culture.

Out our window we obtain our entire education: we see all manner of beliefs, values, attitudes, philosophies—in short, our worldview. We take in enormous detail (which we define as "normal," "right," "real"), but we see it from only one point of view, one perspective. Without a conscious effort to get up and move, we could sit and look at life through that one window forever. Most people do (Allen 1980).

Learning a more holistic perspective does not mean dragging yet another limited and limiting dogma past the one open window. It means acquiring the one insight that would encourage us, when we are ready, to get up and open more windows. Or, in the language of the Popper analogy, turn on more searchlights. In the same way knowledge of the night makes us less threatened by it, this more balanced, comparative view has the capacity to make us more comfortable with our world as it actually is, rather than as any one cultural mythology would have us believe.

"Anthropology" is defined here as an attitude that filters the way we see everythng else in life. It may shed some light on how anthropology can help bring this shift in perception to media information if I share some of my argument to convince a group of anti-academic journalists and ultra-academic anthropologists to allow a combination of the two disciplines during my student days in the late 1960s and early 1970s. I should point out the views expressed do not necessarily represent those of the anthropology community.

"WHENCE IT CAME"— A PHILOSOPHICAL UNDERSTANDING

In that mid-Vietnam War, moon-landing, suddenly globally and ecologically conscious era, many sensed an urgent need for the general citizenry—the people who make decisions about our common futures—to become sensitized to the kind of perspective I had come to associate with anthropology.

I was struck by the logic of reframing many of the mental tools I was learning from anthropology into the new global context. Actually, the essence of anthropology, its anthropological perspective, barely needed reframing. It already referred in principle to the more inclusive-sounding "holistic perspective" that taught us to consider a dynamic, interconnected and interdependent whole in order to understand fragmented parts of it.

In the early 1970s, exclusionism and reductionism—whether in the form of segregation, colonialism, androcentrism, Cartesian logic, or even detached analytical paradigms and rigidly separate disciplines—were giving way to realizations of inclusivity and wholeness. It was the era of "movements" for civil rights, African independence, ecology, equal rights for women and of holistic ideas bursting into our consciousness from such diverse places as "new" physics, ancient Eastern religions, and poetic metaphors like the "spaceship earth" and "global village." Following in the wake of these came a movement toward interdisciplinary studies, and the seedbed for media anthropology was prepared.

It is not surprising that those of us who were at the time learning to see holistic principles applied by anthropology to "whole" cultures were quick to notice—with encouragement from such visionaries as anthropologist Gregory Bateson and futurist R. Buckminster Fuller (not to mention Albert Einstein)—they also applied to any whole, from subparticles of atoms to the universe itself.

Anthropology's call for a relativistic point of view among cultures, meaning that everything within the whole has its own place and function, became translated into a sense of the necessity for an organic kind of balance and mutuality within any system.

The anthropological methods of comparison and participant observation had always urged us to transcend an innate "culture blindness," as anthropologist Edward T. Hall described it. They called on us more mindfully to experience the process and context of "reality" and "truth" rather than accept any one ethno-, chrono-, or anthropocentric version of it, even those versions we hold most dear. These methods and the theories behind them also showed us dynamic but discernible patterns within the essential diversity of culture and nature, helping us see our individual and collective positions in the world more clearly. I realized that an awareness of the consistencies as well as the diversity could give me some grounding for the morass of seemingly random and incoherent details suddenly made visible by the new communications, transportation, and other world-shrinking technologies and that such a perspective had the capacity to make people less fearful of differences and, therefore, less rigid and reactionary toward them.

Even paleoanthropology had lessons for the new global era, with its evidence of the necessity for generalization and adaptability to survive in a changing environment. It was natural to notice that these concepts applied to the human intellect, as well as to physical evolution. From this I learned, among other things, that rigid rules designed for a small, status quo world were no longer adequate for survival and also that although we can never again be comforted by the illusion that we have all of the specific answers we think we need, we can build a "knowledge general" framework that can give us the flexibility to see what is essential and what is detail so we can adapt.

Perhaps most importantly, in allowing its human subjects to be their own "experts," I realized anthropology respected the value of collaborating with the environment rather than trying always to overpower it. Much to the horror of our traditional, isolated, and, yes, authoritarian grandfathers, a whole generation began to learn the value of diversity and to understand the need for open-mindedness and an acceptance of ambiguity. Much to their chagrin, we began to "question authority" as a matter of policy.

In December 1968, when human beings saw photographs of our planet, our "spaceship earth," for the first time—and, within a few years, began witnessing the common, global impact of acid rain, nuclear reactor spills, ozone and rain forest depletion, and so on—it dawned on some of us that as many of our fellow U.S. and global citizens as possible needed to learn, as quickly as possible, the meaning and consequences of holism. This is when the media became essential to public education and to media anthropology.

"As important as formal education is, its influence sometimes does not change attitudes or improve understanding until generations have passed," wrote William Hachten in *The World News Prism* (1981, 7). "In immediate terms, the flow of information and news throughout the globe will have greater impact on the world's ability to understand its problems and dangers and somehow respond to them."

Largely because of the new communications and transportation technologies, we suddenly lived in a new world. Instead of canoes, war clubs, the coconut wireless, and "talking story" in our own backyards, almost overnight we had jets, nukes, satellites, and television capable of linking together the entire globe in an instant. Lots of us began to see that those things anthropology taught us about interconnectedness and interdependence in small, isolated cultures—about coexisting with finite resources in very close, delicately balanced quarters—also operated on a global scale and, to take this idea a step further toward media anthropology, that perspectives available from anthropology had the potential both to calm and to enlighten a deeply threatened general public.

It was exciting to realize the discipline of anthropology had evolved an awareness of the balanced, contextual perspective so desperately needed in the new environment. The task, then, became finding ways to expose as many citizens as possible to its transformational perspectives—even those people who, like the comfortable, myopic satirist Trillin, did not want to know.

In more isolated and innocent times, preceding what communications researcher Colin Cherry called the "threat and promise" of the communications revolution, perhaps traditional anthropology, traditional journalism, and traditional education did reach "enough" people with sufficient speed (Cherry 1971). But not anymore.

It was a logical step to notice that the new communications technologies, which played such a major part in turning our world into the visibly unified whole Marshall McLuhan called a "global village," could also be used to reach global citizens with the information and insights that could help all of us live in it more safely.

At the time, we did not know if anthropologically oriented information would be embraced by the general public or if traditional anthropologists and communicators could cooperate long enough to provide it. Those of us working to combine the two professions did not know one another and didn't know that our work connected with other holistically focused movements. But, in retrospect, it seems that a synergistic alliance between anthropology and journalism—for the purpose of addressing an almost palpable need for a culturally aware, globally conscious public—was "an idea whose time had come."

"THE USE OF ENCHANTMENT"— A PSYCHOLOGICAL UNDERSTANDING

Can anthropologically oriented information help us achieve a more culturally aware and globally conscious general public? Although this is an area for further media anthropological research, a similar idea proposed by the late psychologist Bruno

Bettelheim in relation to fairy tales suggests that it can. Bettelheim said in *The Uses of Enchantment* (1977, 61),

> A young child's mind contains a rapidly expanding collection of often ill-assorted and only partially integrated impressions: some correctly seen aspects of reality, but many more elements completely dominated by fantasy. Fantasy fills the huge gaps in a child's understanding which are due to the immaturity of his thinking and his *lack of pertinent information*. Other distortions are the consequence of inner pressures which lead to misinterpretation of the child's perception. (italics added)

Exchange the word *child* for *people* and remember all individuals continue to grow and mature throughout life, and the above paragraph may be reread as a psychological argument for the use of anthropologically oriented information as the basis for a holistic perspective.

Our minds do contain a "rapidly expanding collection of ill-assorted and only partially integrated impressions." Largely due to our "lack of pertinent information," we have huge gaps in our understanding that are filled with fantasies about ourselves and our world—sometimes in the form of curiosity and hope, but often in the form of prejudice and fear.

There is currently a tremendous lack of what Bettelheim termed "pertinent information" that reaches the general public. Our awareness of unfamiliar peoples of the world and our knowledge of, and sensitivity to, unfamiliar ideas are limited at best, and the gaps in our knowledge are filled with distortions about them.

The information and insights of anthropology could be catalytic to certain kinds of affective developments in our minds in the same way Bettelheim argues that fairy tales affect the development of the mind.

Fairy tales are nonthreatening because they are removed from ordinary reality by devices such as beginning with, "Once upon a time" or "In a far away land." By removing this "pertinent information" (albeit in symbolic form) from direct association to immediate, possibly threatening, situations or thoughts—while, in fact, dealing with universal human concerns—a tale can affect development through the subconscious.

Children are not forced to apply tales to their own situation on a conscious level if they aren't ready to do so, but, as they are able and when they are ready (and, importantly, if the information is available to them), the message can seep in.

In the same way, anthropology can remove us from the immediate situation of our lives by saying, "In Outer Mongolia" or "Where people live in grass huts." But the information therein can act as a mirror. Most human dilemmas are universal, and alternative means of viewing them can sometimes be accepted in a "fantasy" or "exotic" setting where they might not be in a more ordinary setting. Like fairy tales, anthropologically oriented information presented through the mass media is noncoercive. But, if it is available, when people are ready, the message can seep in.

Bettelheim said fairy tales exist so that the story is not placed in time or place of external reality but in a state of mind—that of the young in spirit. Being placed there, he said, "fairy tales can cultivate this spirit better than any other form of literature" (Bettelheim 1977, 62). In a similar way, anthropologically oriented information can cultivate a more flexible spirit, better able to adapt to change and more willing to accept differences and ambiguities (Allen 1980).

"MANY IDEAS IN MANY HEADS"—
A POLITICAL UNDERSTANDING

In 1820 Thomas Jefferson wrote: "I know of no safe depository of the ultimate powers of the society but the people themselves; and if we think them not enlightened enough to exercise their control with some discretion, the remedy is not to take it from them but to inform their discretion" (Fulbright 1979).

It should be becoming clear to even the most separatist practitioners of anthropology, journalism, and, in fact, public education that information needs of today's world make it imperative that they join forces for some purposes. Despite the jet-propelled development of a global consciousness among international politicians and entrepreneurs since World War II, in reality, cultural awareness remains limited to a few citizens directly affected by the new global environment. In a world where information is increasingly translated into power, this becomes a very real concern for advocates of participatory democracy.

As noted, the people on whom we depend for our image of the world are primarily journalists. They select, from the total universe of material that exists on any given day, the small bit they will tell us based on their working definition of "news." Without going into the "what is news" debate, it is safe to say that what traditionally has made news in America has included little information that was intended to give us a global or cultural perspective or show us the interconnectedness of things.

What journalists have not done—and, in fairness, did not do because no one saw any need to do it—is tell us about one another and our environment so we could learn about global balance and develop a sense of our own proportional place within it. Thus, in spite of the new sensitivity to interdependence by a few, the average citizen (including the average journalist and politician) is not aware of, does not understand, and certainly cannot participate effectively in an integrative form of world affairs. This limited picture of the world has created an educational vacuum that leaves most people, including most voters, ill-equipped to make critical decisions affecting our common futures. Following that, it makes most of us increasingly fearful of the tremendous amount of power relegated to the few people with access to information (Allen 1980).

Anthropology is based on a systems view that says to understand anything, parts must be considered in terms of the whole and that these "parts" are of relative value. Journalism exists for the purpose of having an informed public. Media anthropology synthesizes aspects of both journalism and anthropology to create an alternative method of gathering and presenting information that can help fill the educational vacuum, not with more detail but more perspective.

"Perspective" is defined in Webster's as "a view of things in their true relationship or relative importance." Anthropological perspective implies a holistic perspective of the world and where one connects with it. It carries with it the underlying belief that if this "way of seeing" is internalized, it can overlay interpretation of all other information, encouraging one to view it in broader contexts and, thus, make better choices about it.

Just as journalists are finding themselves "in the right place at the right time" to provide the communications skills and channels for global perspective building, so anthropologists are beginning to recognize the potential of anthropology's holistic perspective for building a more realistic frame of reference through which to view media information (Allen 1980).

DOING MEDIA ANTHROPOLOGY

One way to share anthropological perspectives through the media, or "do" media anthropology, is for traditionally trained anthropologists to assume some responsibility for an informed public and learn to use the media. If they do, they can share information and insights that can be catalysts for a holistic frame of reference with the vast majority of people who will never seek culture awareness information or other anthropological perspectives in an academic setting.

Although this is the most typical form of media anthropology practiced today (and the form largely represented in this volume), few anthropologists participate, primarily because, like scientists and other academics, anthropologists have shied away from "informing" the general citizenry for fear of losing academic credibility. By tradition, that job belongs to journalists, and anthropology curricula still do not include communications training.

A notable, if isolated, genre of early anthropology-through-the-media, however, created by gifted anthropologist/communicators, has existed, particularly since World War II; of that, Margaret Mead's work is the best known. Most contributors to this volume practice this form of media anthropology, and—like Mead, Clyde Kluckhohn, Ruth Benedict, Gregory Bateson, Marvin Harris, William Beeman, Walter Goldschmidt, and a few others—they are pioneers among professional anthropologists in their efforts.

Another way to practice media anthropology is to train traditional journalists in the fine points of anthropology and let them continue to do the communicating. The fact is, until now, journalists are the people who have told most of us everything we know about the world, by default, as a result of the professional anthropologists' refusal to associate themselves with the mass media. Foreign correspondents, international wire editors, science writers, and such magazines as *National Geographic* are prominent examples. The advent of cable television and other public information technologies will expand exponentially this kind of presentation. However, the quality of the method is uncertain, most would agree, as journalists rarely, if ever, have training in anthropology or even geography.

Media anthropology is a new alternative. In this age when our interpendence is made clearer every moment and when the mass media have become filters for our worldview, there is dire need for knowledgeable and sensitive media communicators. We need information-bearers who have achieved and can share broad perspectives on global issues, an appreciation of people from myriad backgrounds, and a more grounded and honest knowledge of one's culture and oneself. Who better to assume this new role than professionals knowledgeable about both communication and culture?

With training in both anthropology and communications, media anthropologists can do the kind of comparative, holistic research and analysis traditionally associated with anthropology and also communicate directly with the public by doing jobs traditionally reserved for journalists. Not every student of anthropology or journalism and communications studies will want to pursue this option, but media anthropology can become a valuable public education/information option of both fields.

Many anthropologists and future anthropologists could learn to communicate through media channels and apply their anthropological skills to current events and contemporary issues. Many journalists and future journalists could learn the methods and perspectives of anthropology.

I suggest that if the closeness of our world demands a more inclusive vision than our ancestors needed (even a generation ago), then it is now time to train a new kind of scientist/communicator. That is the purpose of media anthropology.

A SUGGESTED STRUCTURE FOR MEDIA ANTHROPOLOGY

Two branches of media anthropology seem to be forming: an applied branch, with a direct and an indirect division, and a re-

What is Media Anthropology?

search branch (see Figure 2.2). This volume focuses on the applied branch.

Eiselein and Topper (1976) envisioned a similar structure. As Eiselein reiterated (personal communication, 1990), he believes media anthropology involves these concentrations:

1. The use of mass media to communicate anthropological findings, insights, and theories to a nonanthropological public.
2. The use of media as a tool for directed change.
3. The study of media as an important part of the sociocultural integration of a society. This study includes content analysis, audience analysis, and analysis of the function of media within the society.
4. The use of media as a research tool.

Under the framework suggested in the Figure 2.2, Topper and Eiselein's first two activities fall into the applied category; the last two activities cluster under the research branch.

Figure 2.2
The Two Branches of Media Anthropology

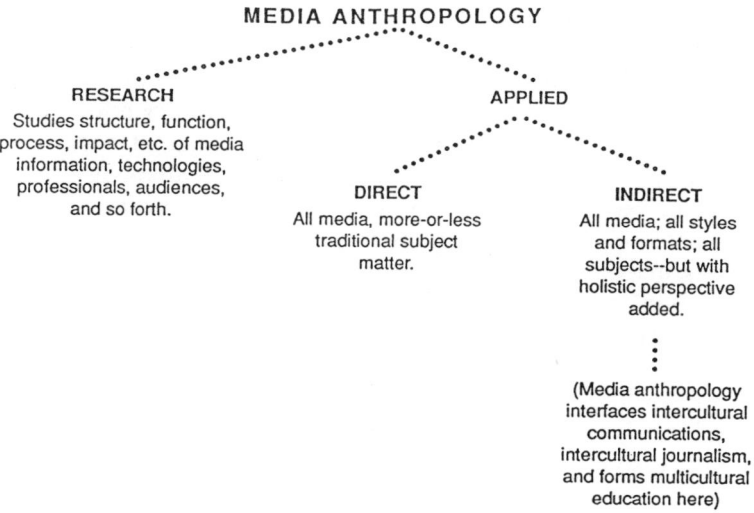

RESEARCH: THE ANTHROPOLOGY OF COMMUNICATION

The research branch of media anthropology brings the methodological and theoretical grounding of anthropology to bear on the structure, function, process, impact, and other aspects of communication and communications technologies. This includes the news and information, the cultures of communications professionals and their audiences, and so forth.

Within the area of international news, for example, international correspondents, the Washington Press Corps, international wire editors, a few institutional press officers, and a very few other information "gatekeepers" play critical roles in our individual and collective worldview. From the millions of happenings that occur each day these journalists select less than 1 percent of the information to pass along to the rest of us, and from these fragments of information most of us form our opinions of peoples of the world and other topics traditionally associated with anthropology. Who are these communicators? How do they see their world? Who are their audiences? How does advertising impact their work? How do communications technologies impact on our lives?

As Eiselein suggests, media anthropology incorporates all of the quantitative and qualitative methods of anthropology and communications studies. Research media anthropology goes beyond traditional communications media studies, however, particularly in its methodology of gathering information and in the theoretical basis for organizing knowledge (Lett 1989).

The research branch of media anthropology will be the topic of another book. However, my own doctoral fieldwork on international news flow among the islands of the South Pacific illustrates one of the many forms media anthropological research may take. My research combined qualitative field interviews with island journalists, quantitative data collection, and a comparative analysis of island newspapers with dissemination of some of the results through the mass media as well as normal academic outlets. As anthropological method stipulates, my research also included living in the Pacific for 15 months and acting as a participant observer in the milieu of international/cultural journalism by serving as assistant editor on an inter-island publication.

This kind of in-depth observation and mixing of (anthropological and journalistic) methodologies is one way media anthropologists can help make information gathered by research projects more accurate and, then, more accessible.

APPLIED: THE COMMUNICATION OF ANTHROPOLOGY

Applying media anthropology implies systematically injecting the dynamic of the holistic perspective available from anthropology into information in any form and through all media.

The function of the *direct or academic division* of the applied branch is to communicate anthropological information and insights through media channels in widely acceptable styles and formats, but through more or less traditional anthropological subject matter. This form has evolved within traditional anthropology and has close parallels with such other subdisciplines of anthropology as practicing anthropology, humanistic anthropology, and visual anthropology. Most contributors to this volume practice this form of media anthropology, as do most other widely known anthropologists.

In the direct division, anthropologists are still acting in the role of anthropologists, but they are using the media as tools.

In the more *indirect division*, media anthropologists—with training in both anthropology and communications—may assume a role traditionally associated with the media. Rather than focusing only on anthropological subject matter per se, it seeks to expose people to information that can generate a more universal perspective, leaving form and substance up to the individual media anthropologist. Some of the material is traditional in its anthropological subject matter, but some of it is not.

As I see it, this indirect, informal division of the applied branch will become a legitimate and important form of media anthropology because this more artistic form can reach that enormous portion of the global citizenry that reads nothing beyond the daily newspaper and listens to nothing except the popular media. It addresses a population that would not seek traditional anthropological subject matter or other perspective-building information, even in the most accessible forms and styles. Indirect applied media anthropology is defined to include the work of trained anthropologists using a full range of subject matter and forms (videos, poetry, popular film, business publications, novels, and the news, to name a few) and perhaps even to bring into the discipline the anthropologically sound work of such nonanthropologists as selected journalists and other communicators.

As with any profession, to be valid and reliable, most media anthropology will come from professionals trained to produce it systematically. However, to make use of the talent that is already out there, if a music video or a Broadway play shares substantively accurate anthropolgical perspectives, the profession of media anthropology needs to find a way to include them.

Journalists play a particularly important part in the indirect form because the journalist and other media communicators set the daily agenda for our worldview.

In fact, it is easier to conceptualize the informal form of media anthropology as something professional communicators—including popular authors, artists, and journalists—would "do," because, in fact, they are the ones whom we see doing it because anthropologists won't. One way to imagine the indirect and nonacademic form of media anthropology is to think what our newspapers would look like if Margaret Mead or Laura Bohannon or Marvin Harris—or an unnamed media anthropologist with training in journalism and anthropology and with a commitment to perspective-building education—had been sitting at the New York wire desk of the Associated Press for the past 50 years; or how the nightly news agenda, selected by national and local broadcasters, would be altered if the writers and editorial "gatekeepers" were sensitized to an anthropological perspective. In this area of contextual and multiperspective information the distinctions among such separate disciplines as anthropology, journalism, public education, multicultural education, and intercultural communications blur and media anthropology naturally occurs.

Good, substantively sound examples of this kind of media anthropology that occur outside traditional anthropology include V. S. Naipaul novels, Ursula K. LeGuin science fiction, Tony Hillerman mysteries; popular movies such as *E.T.* and *The Dead*

What is Media Anthropology?

Poets Society; some of the new cable-TV videos, such as "Millennium"; and, importantly, the work of many international correspondents and such other journalistic works as selected PBS programs by Bill Moyers and National Public Radio pieces from Africa by Daniels Wordling and many others.

What could this odd amalgam of information possibly have in common? In a variety of ways, which gives media anthropology its exciting breadth and also its amorphous appearance, all of these communicators present material meant to broaden our perspective of the world and our place in it. Through the use of storytelling techniques and metaphors that work like poems, these communicators shake us out of our familiar way of seeing. In some cases, they increase our awareness of how culture acts like a blueprint to limit our vision (*Dead Poets Society* and the adults in *E.T.*); in some they broaden our intercultural understanding (Hillerman, Naipaul, many of the journalists and broadcasters); and sometimes they help us glimpse that "God's-eye" view of our life that can give us insight into where we fit into the cosmos. LeGuin (who is the daughter of renowned anthropologist Alfred Kroeber and *Ishi* author Theodora Kroeber) writes science fiction, for example, that could as well be called "space anthropology" because she gives us a perspective on our own lives through stories about "other worlds." *E.T.* tells us we don't need to fear and kill otherworldly aliens just because they are not like us.

It should be emphasized that, although the above examples are of high "academic" quality, journalists and other nonanthropologists produce anthropologically oriented information, with varying degrees of accuracy and audience acceptance, every day. With no media anthropologists to provide it, a growing number of entrepreneurs and adventurers, as well as pseudoscientists and philosophers, have stepped in to fill the void. With the proliferation of such communications tools as computers, video cameras, and cable television stations, this trend is certain to increase in the future.

The only real question for anthropologists at this point is, will we be involved—not just with media tools but with daily journalism and other kinds of informal media communications— to provide some training, standards, and quality control, or will we be bystanders? If we choose not to be involved, by default, this powerful public education function will be left to anyone with a pencil, an imagination, and media access.

REFERENCES

Allen, Susan L. 1975. "Predicting Reader Interest in Anthropology Column." *Journalism Quarterly* 52 (Spring): 124-128.
_____. 1980. "Media Anthropology: Concept and Pacific Islands Case Study." Ph.D. diss. University of Kansas, Lawrence.
_____. 1984. "Media Anthropology: Building a Public Perspective." *Anthropology Newsletter* 25: 6.
_____. 1989. "Training in Media Anthropology." *Anthropology Newsletter* 30 (May): 15.
Bettelheim, Bruno. 1977. *The Uses of Enchantment*. New York: Vintage Books.
Cherry, Colin. 1971. *World Communication: Threat or Promise?* Palo Alto, CA: Wiley Interscience.
Eiselein, E. B., and Martin Topper. 1976. "Media Anthropology." *Human Organization* 35 (June): 111-220.
Fulbright, J. William. 1979. "The Legislator as Educator." *Foreign Affairs* 57: 719-732.
Hachten, William A. 1981. *The World News Prism*. Ames: Iowa State University Press.
Lett, James. 1989. "Anthropology and Television." *Anthro-Journalism* 1 (October): 2.
McLuhan, Marshall. 1962. *The Gutenberg Galaxy*. Toronto: University of Toronto Press.
Smith, Huston, 1976. *Forgotten Truth: The Primordial Tradition*. New York: Harper & Row.
Winokur, Jon. 1987. *The Portable Curmudgeon*. New York: New American Library.

Chapter 3

The Anthropologist as Magazine Writer

Cynthia Lollar

INTRODUCTION

When Margaret Mead began writing a monthly column for *Redbook* magazine in 1961, she was already the country's most famous media anthropologist. She had long believed that well-researched anthropological insight could contribute to a better world beyond the ivy-covered walls of academe. For years since the publication of her first book, *Coming of Age in Samoa*, Mead had written articles on everything from raising children for *Parents Magazine*, to mother-daughter relationships for *House Beautiful*, to the lives of American soldiers in England during World War II for *The New York Times Magazine*.

But as Mead's popularity rose, so did the number of her critics. Her efforts at educating the public came to be seen by many within the academic community as pandering, as if casting her ideas in language suitable for general consumption somehow reduced the value of the original scholarship.

That scorn lingers today in many academic circles as something of a taboo against the popularization of scientific ideas. It is a taboo not unlike the menses taboo as it is practiced in some societies, in which menstruating women are sequestered so as not to overwhelm the magical powers of men with their touch.

Likewise, too many scientists seem to think that the integrity or "magic" of science is lost when touched by everyday idiom and that participating in the making of public opinion compromises their position as scientists or lowers their stature as serious researchers.

Media anthropologists dare to break the popularization taboo and share what they are learning about human thought and behavior with the world at large. Besides Mead, some of the field's brightest stars have successfully written for the general public and maintained their scholastic reputations, including Gregory Bateson, Ashley Montagu, Clyde Kluckhohn, Ruth Benedict, Marvin Harris, Oscar Lewis, Lionel Tiger, Richard Leakey, Melvin Konner, and Loren Eiseley.

Anthropologists working without the protective cloak of wider fame have also bridged the gap between research and public knowledge: Thomas Schroder, trained in anthropology at the University of Florida, is the executive editor of *Tropic*, the Sunday magazine of the *Miami Herald* newspaper; Michael H. Agar, a professor at the University of Maryland and author of the ethnographic textbook *The Professional Stranger*, has contributed to such magazines as *Smithsonian, Trucks,* and *American Way*; and writer and anthropologist Beryl Lieff Benderly has written numerous popular articles and books, including one on the meaning of gender.

In my own work as a media anthropologist with more than a decade's experience in the field of magazines, I have learned firsthand the difficulties and rewards of funneling anthropological knowledge into the popular press. I have written about the anthropology of acquired immunodeficiency syndrome (AIDS), the cross-cultural reverberations of that universal notion "home," and the myriad ways the weekend is experienced and understood around the world. I have written about these topics, but not every article has gotten into print. Many editors retain the stereotyped image of anthropologists as experts in the exotic rather than as competent commentators on the everyday world their readers inhabit.

Still, there is perhaps no better medium than magazines through which anthropologists can share their hard-won wisdom with a larger public sorely in need of some global, intercultural perspective. I am convinced that anthropologists can be doing much more to reach a broader audience with their ideas, thereby improving everyone's understanding of the global village in which we now live. All it takes is learning how. In the rest of this chapter, we explore answers to such questions as:

- What is so special about magazines and why is this effort important?
- What exactly do anthropologists have to offer that sets them apart from other magazine contributors?
- What do anthropologists need to know about magazines in order to "go native" (i.e., get published)?

THE IMPORTANCE OF MAGAZINES

Why should anthropologists consider magazines as a potential forum for their ideas? For one thing, there are more than 11,000 of them in the United States alone. In the past 20 years there has been an explosion of special-interest magazines, including those devoted to computers, pets, food, business, music, health, fitness, conservation, psychology, fishing, aging, travel, plumbing, religion, and farming. At the same time, there remain some strong contenders for the attention of broad-minded readers in the form of general-interest magazines like *Harper's*, *The Atlantic Monthly*, and *The New Yorker*.

The point is that there is a magazine for just about any subject close to an anthropologist's heart. Perhaps even more appealing is the nature of magazine readers themselves. Unlike their newspaper-reading counterparts, magazine readers expect to spend time with an article—they're browsers, not impulse buyers; grazers, not fast-food junkies. True, a magazine reader expects an infusion of substantive thought in less time than it takes to read a book. But an anthropologist looking for an attentive audience willing to allow him or her more than a catchy headline and a lead paragraph in which to develop an idea has no better friend than the magazine reader.

Often mirroring the reader's generosity is the editor's. While some magazines buy into the conventional wisdom that says readers prefer their information pureed into 800-word spoonfuls of easily digested thought, many magazine editors remain on the lookout for writers who can pack an intellectual punch into a 2,000- to 5,000-word article. What is more, compared to newspapers, magazine articles are usually long enough to say something meaningful but short enough to get points across quickly. Magazines can often better accommodate the depth of detail needed to provide adequate context for anthropological tales—the "thick description" Clifford Geertz wrote about in an essay *Harper's* magazine once excerpted from his book, *The Interpretation of Culture*.

Still, even feature-length magazine articles can prove challenging to an anthropologist accustomed to the more open-ended nature of academic publishing. But there is a kind of liberating discipline to the effort. Reasonable journalistic compression forces the best ideas to the surface of the data, where they can do the most good for the largest number of people.

THE ANTHROPOLOGICAL PERSPECTIVE

Media anthropologists believe there is an anthropological perspective lacking in media coverage that is highly relevant to contemporary experience and to the events that count as newsworthy in a particular culture. That perspective comes from the discipline's epistemological wranglings; journalists, after all, do not usually pester themselves with the question, I know I know something, but how do I know what I know? Instead, anthropology offers a framework for looking at current events in terms of holistic context, the insider's perspective, cultural relativity, ethnographic data, and the importance of symbolic, as well as behavioral, reality.

Holistic Context

Anthropologists know that facts are not "just the facts," in and of themselves. Facts make sense only in relationship to other ideas shared by the group in which the facts are taking place. Without an understanding of the larger picture, facts become warped carriers of meaning. Connections among political, economic, ideational, and physical realities—and among these elements over time—are often neglected by journalistically trained writers.

For example, the nationally reported story about gangs of young Vietnamese men breaking into the homes of other Vietnamese immigrants and terrorizing them into giving up money and valuables has been widely written as an American crime story with a twist: it is a fact that recent Vietnamese immigrants tend to distrust banks and keep much of their wealth at home.

But how about a story that explores this "fact" in its larger context? Why do Vietnamese immigrants distrust banks, and how did they handle wealth in their native country? Are these roving gangs a phenomenon that started here, or was it imported? What is motivating the gangs to form? Poverty? Revenge? A sense of cultural displacement? Do the gangs function in the way police have learned to expect of other American gangs, and what purpose does this function serve? What does this experience tell us about the values and lives of the contemporary American Vietnamese community? How are the victims responding? What ideas and beliefs do they call on to make sense of what has happened to them? The answers to these and similar questions would make a fascinating magazine article.

The Insider's Perspective

"Emic" and "etic" are the jargon anthropologists use to talk to each other about whose point of view is being expressed at any given time: the native's or the observer's. Merely having this awareness—that the viewpoint of the observer is often radically different than, and perhaps fallacious in terms of, the native's viewpoint—is enough to put the media anthropologist on a different plane relative to many traditional reporters.

Reporters typically strive to quote different persons with conflicting views in order to achieve "balance" in a story. But giving voice to the insider's perspective is not just about balance. Instead, the media anthropologist often attempts to knit emic and etic explanations into something of a whole cloth, approximating the truth as she or he understands it in terms the subjects themselves would recognize as having merit. For example, it has been argued that the media in this country fail to represent accurately the world as many African Americans see it, largely because media staffs are dominated by whites with little experience in the black community. There is a role for media anthropologists in the resolution of this problem.

Cultural Relativity

The notion of cultural relativity holds that the beliefs and behaviors of one culture cannot be judged according to the values of another culture—there is no hierarchy of cultures in which one is better or worse than another. At its worst, this notion seems to explain away atrocities like the genocidal behavior of the Khmer Rouge as having risen somehow logically from Cambodian culture in the 1960s. At its best, the theory challenges anyone looking at cultural issues to be critically aware of his or her ethnocentrism, which in most of the United States media amounts to white, male, middle-class standards of speech, thought, and behavior.

Their ability to rattle the cage of readers' ethnocentrism provides anthropologists with a natural "hook" for many potential magazine stories. Editors look for a hook (the point of interest that makes the story stand out from the pack) that will surprise readers and grab their attention. Anthropologists are surrounded by such surprises as a matter of course during fieldwork and data analysis; early on, it is called culture shock, and it provides the anthropologist with her or his best source of information about what is happening. Readers will benefit only when more anthropologists share these surprises with them.

Ethnographic Data

Today's journalism is filled with the stark figures of statisticians and the sizzle of popular opinion surveys. These kinds of "hard" numbers appear authoritative to many editors and readers, understandably so. The social science community itself has moved away from qualitative data gathering in recent years toward a heavier reliance on quantitative strategies. Even anthropologists are debating the scientific validity of the technique that has long been the heart's blood of the discipline: ethnography.

The tension between qualitative and quantitative knowledge is nothing new, and while the theorists argue, a lot of good ethnography is going on domestically and abroad. The strength of ethnography—and its potential appeal to magazine editors—lies in the extended, direct contact an anthropologist often has with the people under study.

There is a subcategory of journalists called "investigative reporters" who, unlike their largely desk-bound and deadline-hounded colleagues, are expected to immerse themselves in their subject's milieu for as long as it takes to "get the story." Investigative reporters are highly respected in their profession. They demonstrate a kind of credible intimacy with their subject unlike that achieved by regular reporters, who rely on telephone interviews and background research for much of their material.

Magazines such as *Mother Jones, Time,* and *The New Yorker* are home to good investigative journalism, thanks to their long production schedules (two to six months as opposed to the daily grind on newspapers) and space allowances. Even newspapers sometimes unleash their reporters for lengthy, on-the-scene reporting. Leon Dash of the *Washington Post* spent more than a year living in the city's poverty-ridden southeast section for an award-winning series on teenage pregnancy (which he later reproduced as a book called *When Children Want Children*).

Because of their comfort with the notion of investigative journalism, many magazine editors are primed to accept an anthropologist's field experience as credible material for a story. In fact, nothing alienates editors more than writers who are unable to support their ideas with some on-the-ground, eyewitnessed events that illustrate points for the reader—just the sort of events that anthropologists are likely to record.

One anthropologist wrote an article for the *New York Times Magazine* on his work among drug addicts in the city. He turned a confrontation among himself, the police, and a couple of his informants into a riveting opening anecdote, even though quite probably the incident was similar to many he witnessed that, taken together, constituted the basis for a more formalized analysis of the area's drug culture. Throughout the rest of the article, he illustrated his larger themes with re-created scenes from his ethnographic work. Ethnography—in the scientific quality of its data and in its more superficial guise of editorial color—is a natural bridge to the minds and hearts of magazine readers.

Symbolic and Behavioral Realities

Most journalists are empiricists. Particularly because they do not have the luxury of spending large amounts of time with the subjects of their stories, journalists learn to rely primarily on what their senses tell them is going on. They concentrate on what people do or what people say they do.

Anthropologists learn to see beyond what people say and do. Those who study symbolic systems or who are at least cognizant of the role of mental constructs in the day-to-day doings of human beings have an advantage over traditional journalists in this regard. Not only are they sensitive to the influence of culture-bound ideas on the behavior of people, but they have the tools to discover and study them and bring them to the attention of readers who might not otherwise grasp their significance in relation to newsworthy events.

The tidal wave of change stemming from communism's fall in Eastern Europe and the Soviet Union is a prime example of where an anthropological perspective can be put to good journalistic use. To many Americans, there seems to be a confusing multitude of ethnic rivalries suddenly erupting in once peaceful countries such as Yugoslavia. Closer to home are the mounting deaths and disquiet in our inner cities. "What are they *thinking* of?" is a common query after yet another round of violence; a good media anthropologist could tell us.

In short, there is such a thing as an "anthropological perspective" that can be a highly productive, engaging way of offering greater understanding of contemporary affairs to the general public. To recap, the characteristics of an anthropological perspective include:

- The placement of the story within a larger societal context.
- An exploration of the culture process at work.
- A sense of the story's relevance and meaning through time (historically) and across space (cross-culturally).

THE WORLD OF MAGAZINES

Applying the anthropological perspective to a magazine article that is well written and salable requires sensitivity to the realities of magazine publishing and a willingness to learn a style of writing different from that normally seen in academic or professional journals. Here are a few aspects of the magazine world that media anthropologists should keep in mind.

Time and Space Constraints

I have mentioned these earlier, but they bear repeating. It takes journalists a long time to become practiced in the art of concise and potent writing under deadline pressure, and for anthropologists schooled in a different style of writing, the effort can be even more daunting. You must squeeze your lengthy fieldwork experiences and post-fieldwork analyses into 5,000 words or less, at the same time choosing which aspects of your work are most relevant to the readers' interests. One trick is to think of your field notes as a house on fire: what ideas *must* you carry out before the house burns down and damns everything to oblivion? (More on writing style later.)

The Reader Comes First

Academic journals present their field's latest research to a community of peers who share a core of knowledge. They do not rely for their fiscal health on mass distribution. The author hopes the article will garner wide attention within the narrow band of his or her profession, but the driving question for him or her is not, What do others want to hear? but rather, What do I want to say?

Mass circulation magazines, on the other hand, survive primarily at the whim of their readers, who share no great body of common knowledge and in truth are more different than alike. So magazine editors look for articles that will appeal to *most* of the readers *most* of the time. In fact, editors tend to reduce this abstract multitude to an intuited sense of the typical reader, and it is this mythical reader (as understood by the reader's surrogate, the editor) to whom would-be writers must slant their articles. While it has been argued that editors often underestimate their readers' intelligence and willingness to be challenged, the cold reality is that writers seeking to sell articles must satisfy the editor that they have something to say that his or her reader wants to hear.

Understand the Market

Lest you fear for your scholarly integrity, know that writing an article with the reader's interests in mind does not require you to twist your ideas around in order to get published. The trick is to find those magazines with readers (i.e., editors) who think your ideas are worthwhile and of interest. How? One way is to look through the most recent edition of *Writer's Market*, a standard reference that lists more than 4,000 potential U.S. markets for fiction, nonfiction, scripts, and even humorous gags. The publications are grouped into categories, and it is a simple matter of reading those listings that sound closest to the kind of audience you would like to reach. Each listing offers a description of the publication (including what kinds of articles it is looking for) and a person's name and address to contact.

However, the guide will not give you enough of a feel for the magazine. Just as you would not presume to publish articles about a culture you had never visited, so you must acquaint yourself with the magazine for which you would like to write. Send a stamped, self-addressed envelope to the contact person listed in the market guide with a request for "writer's guidelines." These will give you more detail about the kind of subject matter, length, and writing style most likely to suit the magazine's tone and objectives. You may also ask for some sample copies of the magazine if you cannot find back issues in your library (be sure to enclose an appropriately sized and stamped self-addressed envelope). Read these issues carefully for clues that will help you translate what you have to say into an article the magazine would be likely to publish.

Once familiar with a magazine, you are ready to write what is called a "query letter." The query letter is a one-page pitch to the editor that (1) presents the "hook" or attention-grabbing point of the story; (2) summarizes what the article will contain, how you will get the information, and why you are the perfect person to write it; and (3) shows something of your flair for writing. There are plenty of good books and articles about what goes into an effective query letter (check back issues of *Writer's Digest* magazine), so I will not elaborate here. But knowing *what* you want to say and knowing *how* to say it in good, nonfiction style are very different. You may first need to change some basic writing habits you picked up on your way to becoming an anthropologist.

Learn How to Write . . . Again

More than many scientists, anthropologists are accustomed to putting their ideas down on paper in narrative form. But as a media anthropologist, you must be able to step away from whatever format and tone are expected by your field's academic journals and, instead, express your ideas with an engaging vibrancy and passion.

Magazine editors often talk about wanting "voice" in the article they publish. Voice is the key stylistic element in good writing because it gives the illusion of a speaker behind the printed words, a speaker whose personality somehow emerges from between the lines to stand beside the reader and bring the narrative to life. Academic and professional journals have a voice that is appropriate to them; it is the voice of one restrained by figures and graphs, sober and passionless, mind without body. This kind of writing style subsumes the voice of the author within what rightly should be the larger authority—the data.

Magazine readers care about your data, but only insofar as they are enabled to comprehend them through an energetic narrative told in a lively voice. Contrary to the inverse relationship that seems to exist in the minds of too many scientific authors, data do not lose significance by gaining readability (see, e.g., Stephen Jay Gould or Lewis Thomas). In fact, you may find, as did Michael Agar of the University of Maryland, that your academic writing benefits greatly from the rigors of writing clearly and well for a lay audience.

One way of releasing your voice from the necessary restraints of academic writing is to write your magazine article as if it were a letter to a friend unfamiliar with your topic. The kind of conversational, warm tone we often practice in letters is perfect for inviting readers to take the points of your article to heart.

Other writing habits you may have to overcome include the tendency to qualify each statement or opinion and to cite the authors whose work helped you reach the insights you are now presenting as your own.

Anthropologists, with their sensitivity to holistic context, must in their scientific writings carefully delineate the various ways a particular event might possibly be interpreted, regardless of the one interpretation for which they may be making a case. Societies and cultures, after all, are not like DNA; they cannot be mapped out and labeled according to mechanistic rules. It is important to show other scientists how you reached a certain conclusion and that you thoughtfully considered rival hypotheses before rejecting them.

Magazine readers do not really care *how* thoughtfully you considered all that you considered or who influenced you in your thinking. The important thing to them is *what you know*. Remember, you are the expert in the eyes of the editor (if you have written your query letter right), and that is how you will be presented to the readers. By "expert," editors do not mean the one and only authority on your subject, just a credible spokesperson with a noteworthy opinion to express. So relax and enjoy the forum.

Of course you will need to marshal evidence for your conclusions, but not to the degree required by your colleagues. But beware of oversimplification. Think of this process not as a dilution of your knowledge, but as a distillation for the intelligent, lay reader.

Finally, there is the matter of certain literary techniques that, while as unwelcome in academic journals as chatty parishioners in church, greatly enhance a magazine article's appeal and effectiveness. These include dramatic tension, scene setting, dialogue, and characterization—all the elements that keep you moving through a good novel at the beach.

Much has been written about the controversial merits of so-called literary journalism, a style that arose in the 1960s in which the techniques of fiction are applied to the realities of nonfiction.

(For examples read *The Literary Journalists*, edited by Norman Sims.) But you should know that, at the least, editors expect your article to be carried forward by dramatic or telling anecdotes drawn from your own experiences or those of others and redrawn as ministories complete with a limited degree of setting, characters, and conflict resolution.

Other Tricks of the Trade

Given that much of what anthropologists do is study the ordinary lives of ordinary people, recognizing the stuff of drama may seem difficult at first. But Richard Leakey was not born with an eye for ancient hominid bone fragments buried in a dusty gully; he learned to recognize the treasures he was looking for. So can you.

A good way to train yourself to recognize the dramatic vignettes hidden within your data or experience is simply to become conscious of what you like about your favorite books, fiction as well as nonfiction. How is dialogue used, and when? What details about people serve to sharpen images of them in your mind? When does a description about the surrounding environment advance the meaning of a story?

Consider brushing up on your writing skills or learning new ones by taking a writing course at a nearby university or community college. A good instructional book series is the one produced by Writer's Digest Books; ask your librarian for help in tracking them down as they are often not available except from the publisher itself. Another excellent guide is William Zinsser's *On Writing Well*.

You might also consider joining a writer's group. Usually these are informal gatherings of people whose writing efforts range widely, from the amateur to the professional, and they would almost certainly welcome an anthropologist interested in producing material for a general audience. Ask for references from the nearest university journalism or English department, your local librarian or arts group, or even the editorial staff of your local newspaper.

If your writing already hums and your ideas crackle with contemporary appeal, think about finding an agent. Usually agents help those with book-length manuscripts find publishers, but some top-notch magazines such as *Esquire* also prefer to take on new contributors via their agents. An agent can help you fine-tune your writing for a broader audience, the way a good editor would (although unlike an editor, the agent gets a cut of your manuscript's selling price). *Writer's Market* lists author's agents from around the country, and certainly your local writer's group would know of respected and effective agents in your area.

Finally, if an editor rejects your queries with kind and encouraging words, call him or her and cultivate a rapport with him just as you would a key informant. Become the editor's student and learn what you can do to place an article in his or her magazine. Editors who will take phone calls and personally answer queries are invaluable to a would-be writer; use them as an inside source of information to advance your understanding of the magazine publishing world and your place in it.

Getting Started

As you can see, a media anthropologist writing for magazines wears two hats: scientist and journalist. The former hat may always fit more comfortably than the latter. If so, that is OK. You do not have to be Margaret Mead to be an excellent media anthropologist. The steps outlined above are enough to get you started on the road to magazine journalism within the realm of anthropology. As in anything, you will learn more as you go along.

I applaud you for making this journey. Writing for the public is not honored in most academic settings as a professional credential, and you cut against the grain when you try. But you will nonetheless find great pleasure and intellectual reward in discovering ways to communicate your ideas (and perhaps even your dreams) to people hungry for new understanding of a rapidly changing world. What more can anthropology offer?

Chapter 4

The Anthropologist as Editorial Writer

Randolph Fillmore

"Will you ever run for office?" I asked.
He thought for a moment.
"No," said George Will, nationally syndicated columnist and well-known political conservative. "Right now I have the greatest job in the world."
Will was my first interview and I was eager to catch every word on my notepad as he outlined his daily routine and spoke with warmth about his freedom to write, his freedom to express his opinion. I was a serious undergraduate in anthropology dabbling in an intro-level journalism course. After his speaking engagement on campus I, cub reporter, had been somehow delegated to interview George Will for the school newspaper.
Although my editorial-self rarely agreed with him, my reporter-self was somewhat star-struck interviewing George Will. My anthropological-self and writer-self were thinking that yes, he just might have the greatest job in the world. In fact, the freedom to travel, research, and write was a perfect job for an anthropologist. Whether I agreed with Will's political convictions or not, his ideas about his world's greatest job stuck with me, and by the time I started graduate work in medical anthropology I was writing and publishing in newspapers across the country. The unlikely combination of an anthropological, nonbiased approach

and the overtly opinionated subjectivity of the editorial seemed to find a proper place—the op-ed page (opposite the editorial page).

Everyone's carefully articulated editorial opinion—syndicated or nonsyndicated writers with political or social agendas, retired schoolteachers with a literary bent and flourish, or presidents of associations—has a place of growing importance in U.S. newspapers. Since the 1960s, the op-ed page has been an open arena where writers congregate to express their hearts. Anthropologists, who have unique information about human behavior and its cultural context, should not be left out.

But writing an editorial is mechanically and subjectively a long way from academic writing. While an editorial requires an average investment of only 700-plus well-crafted words, it demands in those 700 words patience, a point, a clear and measured voice to express that point, the ability to make the point in a logical way, and the ability to inform and entertain as well as provoke thought and passion. Both word economy and a well-rounded fund of knowledge are essential. How well rounded? Robert Estabrook of the *Washington Post* said that good editorial writers should know "English, history, political science, economics, natural science, sociology, languages, psychology and philosophy" (Rystrom 1983, 63).

Not anthropology? Perhaps he did not think about it. Too much information, however, is being disseminated in today's media-active world without anthropological notions or points of view being expressed. Newspaper readers are poorer for it. So are we, as anthropologists, poorer for the lack of effort at communicating at large not only what we know but how we know it. Most importantly, we need to communicate why we think the kind of knowledge we possess is important. Editorials are great vehicles for doing that.

Of course, editorial writing is not for all of us. Kenneth Rystrom, in his book *The Why, Who and How of the Editorial Page* (1983), says that editorial writers need to have a wide variety of interests. They need to write in an interesting and convincing manner and have the spirit of the reformer and a solid commitment to principles. Most importantly, the editorial writer must desire to express an opinion. The ability to reason cogently, to be able to reason from the particular to the general as well as from the general to the particular, is important. Perhaps the most important skill is to blend harmonious fact and opinion and do it without preaching.

In times past, editorial writers were passionate and zealous and often the paid mouthpieces of publishers and/or political parties. But today's readers want to make up their own minds about issues and ideas. They do not want truth through fire-tongued revelation as the nineteenth-century stereotype suggests. Passions have muted into points of view; an authoritarian tone has become an educational one. Thus, today's editorial must add something to what appears as hard news and social issues that so often touch on the concerns of anthropologists. On the editorial page, anthropologists can have their say on ethnic issues, urban problems, changing gender roles, war, ritual, teen pregnancy, or drugs.

What it takes to get ideas and views published as editorials is a matter different from what it takes to write them. James J. Kilpatrick, writing in the National Council of Editorial Writers magazine, *The Masthead*, said that the editorials that get published are most often those that use "historical perspectives, comparison and parallel situations, related material and, most importantly, fresh facts" (Rystrom 1983, 46). To Kilpatrick's idea I would add "fresh outlook." Kilpatrick goes on to say that the editorialist's goal is—in 700 words or less—to be "temperate, calm, dignified, forceful, direct, catchy, provocative, stimulating, reasoned, logical, literate, factual, opinionated, conclusive, informative, interesting and persuasive" (Rystrom 1983, 46).

WRITING THE EDITORIAL

Select and Research a Topic

Writing the editorial is a step-by-step procedure that is not so different from any other writing in that it begins with research. First, select and research a topic. Hunting the "news peg," the current story, event, or issue to which you are going to connect and address your efforts, is the first step. When the editorial boards of newspapers meet to discuss future editorials, their concerns are (1) what is the news peg?; (2) is doing an editorial based on it important, and will it add to the news?; and (3) what is our position?

News pegs that touch on matters anthropological should be easy to identify, although they are often found in small articles not on the front page. For example, when I saw a one-column-wide, ten-line-long news item that spoke of a foundation reimbursing a Navajo man for the sheep he paid a traditional healer, I knew that I had an "anthro-journalism" story falling into my lap, one on which I could write an op-ed piece. A phone call to the Phoenix Crime Victim Foundation supplied a few facts. Not all news pegs are so instantly recognizable for anthropologizing upon. But, as regularly as the evening paper follows the morning paper, stories that deserve an in-depth, anthropological slant constantly surface in the news but require searching out.

Determine the Purpose

Once the news peg is selected, the purpose of the editorial is the next consideration. For editorializing in the media anthropological mode, recognizing the anthropological significance and what an anthropologist can say about the news peg should be fairly easy. Of course, stories heavily steeped in interpersonal relations, ethnic strife, changing gender roles, and worldviews on abortion may be easier to address than the closing of the savings and loan association down the street.

Determine the Audience and Select a Tone

The selection of audience and tone can be a problem. Learning to write publishable editorials means reading a substantial number of them—reading them not only to determine the structural common denominators but to find out how successful editorialists think and write, thereby learning how editorial page editors think.

Small percentages of newspaper readership spend any time at all on the editorial pages. Editorial readers are a self-selected group who, as you might imagine, are somewhat better educated than those who do not touch the page. Tone, lexicon, and depth of subject matter should be aimed accordingly. You are not writing for other anthropologists, not even Ph.D.s in other fields, so academically stilted wording is out. Think in economy terms but in well-developed economy. The audience is an educated one who has a general interest in the issues, events, and news of the day, who does not like to be preached to, and who wants its intelligence respected but wants to be educated. An editorial writer's tone must satisfy that desire and need. Of all of the things James Kilpatrick had to say about quality editorial writing, most refer to tone.

Determine a Structure

Determining the structure of your editorial, and therefore the structure of your argument, is easy once you realize that the quality of your lead will determine whether a reader (or editor) will stay with you. One must structurally and thematically invite the reader to continue by placing your argument, your fresh insight, even a piece of your conclusion up front. The lead writing should be clear, crisp, and not in the least nondirectional. You must tell the reader where he or she is going. In other words, the beginning might be the most important part of the editorial.

Write the Beginning

Word economy and a crisp, clear point of view often work well together in a lead. A recent *Washington Post* editorial that my students and I dissected in class was a floundering thing with 43 words in the opening sentence. It was dense, and we all agreed that outside our reading it for the sake of criticism, we would rather have not read it. As editors we would have modified it greatly or sent it back, provided that the author had sent us a self-addressed stamped envelope (SASE). The first sentences are crucial. Write them that way. Let the first sentences set the tone and the tonal structure and allow the structure of the argument to follow cleanly and logically from the lead.

Write the Middle

The weakest spot of the editorial is usually the middle. That is also the weakest place for presenting a central argument. A good structure might be a one that goes from statement, to argument #1, to argument #2, to discussion, to conclusion. The middle should present supporting evidence that your argument, your view, your comparison are logical. A good supportive middle also creates the transition to the conclusion, which needs to be more than, and stronger than, a recapitulation of the original premise or argument stated in the beginning.

Write the End

Your conclusion must leave the reader in one of three frames of mind—complete agreement, vehement disagreement, or thought-provoked and mulling over what you have said. This, too, is how the editorial page editor who reads your piece must react. If he or she reacts otherwise, you may not get into print.

THE EDITORS

To get an editor to read your unsolicited work and consider it for publication it must be immediately apparent to the editor that it will fit the paper's (the editor's) needs. The paper's needs vary. Editors, or their editorial assistants, sort the day's editorials into stacks—those that are an immediately publishable possibility go into one stack, and those to which the editors are lukewarm or that may be relevant depending on how the week's news develops go into another pile; the rejects go in yet another pile. Not long after *Baltimore Sun* op-ed editor Hal Piper put one of my articles in a Saturday edition, I saw him at a writers' social gathering, and I inquired about another piece I had more recently sent him.

"It's in a pile on my desk," Piper said, smiling. I knew by his tone and smile that it was not a reject. I also knew that it was not going to appear in print. He liked it but was not going to run it. He was just keeping it around.

What generally works best for immediate publication rather than for lingering in piles is a well-researched article on local issues or problems. The localness of your issue and your anthropological slant will add to your chances of getting into print. Editors are always looking for fresh insights or ideas and novel ways of looking at a specific issue. When it comes to national or international issues, editors like to stick with writers who can show specialized credentials as well as an interesting perspective. If your area is Latin America, urban problems, or medical anthropology, your best chance in the national market is to speak as an expert in your area.

In learning to be brief, remember that 900 words is normally the optimum length for an op-ed piece, although some papers have space for longer articles of up to 2,500 words in the Sunday editorial section. If your work ends up in the pile of rejects, you will get a rejection letter and your article returned if you have sent a SASE. If you have sent an article to many papers, it is a good idea to keep track of who has rejected it. Besides knowing whether you are getting published or not, by keeping track of the signed rejection notices, you also will be kept informed about who the op-ed editor is. Editors change from time to time. If you elect to use a cover letter with each article, it is good to personalize it because you are, in effect, establishing a relationship with the editor, a relationship that could be a long one. Most editors know that printing good writers regularly enables them to develop over time. In an effort to initiate a relationship I always address the letter to the editor by name where possible, although I know that on larger papers the first and perhaps only person to see my piece will be an editorial assistant. The editorial assistant is the gatekeeper, and if the article pleases the assistant, he or she will send it to the op-ed editor. If your article is accepted, you will normally get a phone call from the editorial assistant, who will want to verify certain information.

Whether you send a cover letter or not, be certain to include your address as well as your home and work telephone numbers along with the article. Include your social security number so that you can be paid. The rate of pay varies. The *Cleveland Plain Dealer* pays $50 per piece while the *Baltimore Sun*, the *Miami Herald*, and the *Los Angeles Heald Examiner* pay $100. The *Des Moines Register* pays $35 while papers like the *New York Times* and *Washington Post* pay over $100 per piece.

You may submit one article to as many papers as you care to. However, I usually send any one article to only one paper per city. If the city has more than one paper, I would wait until the piece is rejected by one before sending it to the other. I know of only two papers, the *Los Angeles Times* and *New York Times*, that require exclusive material. Since I had sent a piece to several papers when the *Los Angeles Times* editorial assistant called me because op-ed page editor Bob Berger was interested in one of my articles, we had to determine if any other paper was going to use it. Fortunately, no other paper had been planning to run it. Unfortunately, the *Los Angeles Times* never ran it either. Rejections are common, but it was nice to be a near miss.

Like academics, newspaper editorial writers and editorial page editors are often regarded as ivory tower dwellers aloof from the reporters and the buzzing newsrooms. The ivory tower stereotype may be based on reality. Editorial writers and editorial page editors often have advanced degrees in journalism or political science, and many have spent years abroad. Hal Piper of the *Baltimore Sun*, for example, before his op-ed editorial appointment, was the *Sun*'s Moscow correspondent. He speaks Russian fluently and has written articles on culture change in the Arctic. Not your average reporter.

Editorial writers should not further the ivory tower stereotype. Trying to woo editors with intellectual bombasticity will not do either. Neither will shallow treatments of the valuable information you have to share.

Besides being smart, editorial page editors have a garden of ripe material from which to choose. Your chances can be improved by giving them good reason to choose your work because a good-looking op-ed page makes them look and feel good.

The best way to get started writing op-ed is to start in another column on the editorial page, the "letters to the editor" column. Good letters are editorials, and writing them is a way to learn to say something succinctly and clearly while paying attention to development and word economy. A few 250-word letters published will make you more comfortable with the 700–900-word limit of the op-ed piece. Small, local papers provide a good testing ground for publishing before you try larger papers, many of which get 100 free-lance op-ed pieces a day as well as pieces from the wire services and the syndicates. Although the competition is stiff for the bigger papers, the anthropological perspective stands out.

The Anthropologist as Editorial Writer 55

Another tack to success is to find a small local paper for which you could be a reporter in your spare (who has it?) time. Most editors let staff writers try their hand at editorials occasionally. While in school I spent a year as a part-time restaurant reviewer for a small local paper (a great way to get dinner on a Saturday night), and I did get a few editorials published during that period. The step up to a larger paper is not impossible once you are experienced. Many full-time editorial writers, even on papers such as the *New York Times* and *Washington Post*, do not come from journalism backgrounds. One of my sources claims that out of 55 candidates hoping to fill an editorial board slot, the *Detroit Free Press* selected "an assistant professor." An assistant professor of what, my source could not recall.

What publishers want from editorial writers and what op-ed editors want especially from free-lancers are "context and perspective." In other words, they want a holistic approach that will place an event or an issue in historical and/or cultural perspective.

This idea is advocated by editorial writer Stephen Rosenfeld when he says, "A good editorialist ought to assert a particular vision of society in which the problem has arisen and the editorial should speak for decency and fairness because certain issues are meant to be met on 'high ground' " (Rystrom 1983, 67). Rosenfeld went on to cite low-level examples that need high-ground editorializing: torture in Brazil and former agriculture secretary Earl Butz's racial comments. Neither issue can be reached on high ground without supplying background. Nor, I would add, can high-ground issues be reached without reference to the values of a people and the value context of the news peg.

In dealing with personal values, *Washington Post* editorialist Colman McCarthy feels that editorials can work a radical change in the way things go in the world. For McCarthy, there is no point in writing any editorial that does not try to bring the reader to another level of consciousness where "an old truth" can be viewed from a different angle and where another route in personal action is the result.

In evaluating the worth of a topic, it is important to realize that what is news and what is not news relate to value systems. News might be thought of as something that either reinforces or contradicts values. The more an issue or event contradicts, reinforces, or reflects values in action (positive or negative based on the value system in which news is contextualized), the more newsworthy the issue or event is. Thus, the news peg that can be identified as having a value-laden basis becomes a better news peg for anthropologizing.

Values also play a role when editors plan their pages. When newspaper editors convene to discuss and decide which of the day's events will be tomorrow's editorial, they meet as a board to decide what news peg they will use, to ask if it is worthy of an editorial, and, to find their position. The op-ed writer must be his or her own editorial board.

When I recently sat in on the editorial board meeting of a large national newspaper, I was surprised to see such positional disagreement among editors. In many cases, once a news peg was selected and judged worthy of elaboration by an editorial, the board argued their position(s) among them until all, or mostly all, agreed on a position. For the op-ed writer, finding a position might be equally difficult, perhaps more difficult, when anthropological training requires a multifocus lens. But defining news, redefining news, and elaborating news out of its ethnocentric structure are the special mission of the anthropologist as op-ed writer. It is a process and a goal that should not be underestimated because of the narrow way in which news is defined and reported.

According to George Will, news organizations, especially those in Washington, define news narrowly. For a columnist in a complicated society there must be more to reporting than collecting the thoughts of, or thoughts about, public officials. "What made Van Gogh a genius," said Will, "was his distinctive way of seeing sunflowers." The "genius" in anthro-journalistic op-ed writing is the distinctive, comparative anthropological evaluation of social behavior in its cultural context. Most of the competition cannot do this. As politically versed writers and thinkers they merely take a personally political or typically Western philosophical position within the frameworks created by all of the politically oriented journalists who have preceded them.

The strength and charm of anthropologist David Kertzer's op-ed piece on the George Bush inauguration were in its tribal comparison and in showing how symbols work to create meaning. He did this humorously and in such a way that readers did not get bogged down in theory.

With a planned event such as an inauguration, plenty of time is available for composing a piece. However, events that are unexpected require finding a position quickly. Overnight, perhaps. Finding a position should not take so long that the value of the news peg lapses. Cliché or not, the fast-paced nature of news requires a quick response. When *USA Today* solicits guest editorials, guests often have only 24 hours to reply. Staying on top of issues cannot be underrated. Even while working on one editorial, one must keep an ear to the ground. On October 19, 1987, I worked hard all day on an article about the stock market. I did not eat or listen to the radio all day, not even in the car when heading to the post office to mail off 20 copies of my new gem. It was not until I was back in the car and switched on the radio that I found that while I was busy discussing predictability in the stock market, it had spent all day crashing. My worthless editorial and $20 in postage crashed with it.

JUST SAY YES TO HEROIN

Occasionally, rather than crash like the stock market, an op-ed piece will take off like a rocket and open "windows of opportunity." For example, after the *Los Angeles Herald Examiner* ran a piece I had written about Senate Bill 67, which seeks to remove the restrictions from heroin's use in cases of terminal cancer, two Los Angeles radio stations called requesting phone interviews. Fortunately I had visited with anthropologist Molly Schuchat about radio interviews and carried off the experience. This increased my commitment to the bill: together with an oncologist who favors heroin's use, I am seeking national coverage for the issue through more radio talk shows. While the physician is able to talk about the pharmacological aspects of heroin's use, I have restricted most of my comments to our cultural biases attached to the word *heroin* and how the biases affect political decision making. In short, I am using an anthropological perspective to advocate something against which I feel there is cultural bias.

Advocacy anthropology is not new, of course. According to

Erve Chambers (1985, 21), anthropology based on an "advocacy-action" model seeks to redress the imbalance in approaches to problem solving by representing perspectives that are often alternative to the perspectives of government policymakers or corporate interests. In lookng at the issue of heroin for terminal cancer pain, I found that lifting restrictions from heroin's use in controlled and specific circumstances met most opposition from lawmakers who harbored fear rather than information. The American Medical Association expresses opposition on an intellectual level, claiming that other drugs, when properly used, are as effective. Terminally ill cancer patients, their families, the American Nurses Association, and many oncologists, people closer to the issue and the pain and farther from politics, disagree.

READER INTEREST

How interested will readers be in editorials written by anthropologists? According to a 1970s study that looked at columns written from an anthropological perspective (Allen, 1975), readers might be as interested in them as they are in editorials and columns written about politics or sports.

The purpose of Allen's 1972 study was to predict reader interest in a syndicated-type newspaper column related to anthropology. Using the Haskins title method as a tool, respondents were provided with booklets that listed titles and subtitles of 18 columns, and, based on the title, they rated on a zero to 100 scale those they were most likely to read (Haskins 1960, 224-230). Interest in selected anthropology titles fell within five degrees of three other high-interest categories: general interest, social comment, and sports. Those within the anthropology categories that ranked highest related to linguistics, physical anthropology, social anthropology, and archaeology. The conclusion was that newspaper readers found anthropological topics interesting and that newspapers provided a good channel for communicating anthropological information. The study concluded with the realistic projection that an actual column should appear in a newspaper before a more valid measure of interest can be determined.

Large syndicates provide newspapers around the country with

columns written by prominent writers such as George Will, William Raspberry, and Ellen Goodman. For anthropologists to join other writers in this competitive business might require syndication after several media anthropologists create a track record. Is it feasible to create a column entitled "Today's Anthropologist" that would provide weekly columns written by anthropologists on a rotating basis? Such a column would provide readers with an anthropological message that they might not be likely to forget. Too, it would provide a media-oriented outlet for anthropology and anthropologists.

REFERENCES

Allen, Susan. 1975. "Predicting Reader Interest in Anthropology Column." *Journalism Quarterly* 52: 124-128.
Chambers, Erve. 1985. *Applied Anthropology*. Englewood Cliffs, NJ: Prentice-Hall.
Haskins, Jack B. 1960. "Pre-testing Editorial Items and Ideas for Reader Interest," *Journalism Quarterly* 37 (Spring): 224-230.
Rystrom, Kenneth. 1983. *The Why, Who and How of the Editorial Page*. New York: Random House.

Chapter 5

The Anthropologist as Newspaper Journalist

Thomas Shroder

I had to force myself to walk into a newsroom for the first time. I was repulsed by the idea of journalism. Shallow, sensationalistic, without context, texture, or subtlety. I thought of journalists as gruff and insensitive, the kind of people who would shout out rude and sometimes ignorant questions and shove their way to a better vantage point at funerals.

My distaste for the profession came as naturally as my affinity for anthropology. Introduction to Cultural Anthropology was my first college elective, chosen because the catalog description appealed to me: "The holistic study of human cultures, with an emphasis on cultural relativism and understanding cultural structures from the inside out." The professor was bearded and droll, a born teacher. His name was Stuart McCrae. Picture Sean Connery in *Medicine Man*. Although in my heart I wanted to write fiction, it was in McCrae's class, not English lit, that I felt at home. My interest in fiction was nothing more than a fascination with the human condition, a desire to explore the mystery of how people behave and maybe even reveal the forces that motivate behavior.

That is exactly what McCrae was up to. In the monographs he assigned there was a theme: cultural traits that we thought of as negative—violence among the Yanamamos, absentee fathers among Caribbean blacks—were actually part of a complex strategy for survival. The idea that even these characteristics were part of the inherent genius of culture—whether participants realized it or not—struck me with the force of revelation.

Before the semester was over I decided I wanted to major in anthropology. I was not thinking about a career. I just wanted to know more. This was several years before I would even consider being a journalist. When I finally walked into the student newspaper office looking for a job, I did it only grudgingly. I had always said I wanted to be a writer, yet I rarely managed to write more than an occasional term paper. I submitted myself to deadlines and angry editors with the grim logic of a man who joins the marines to get in shape.

It was then that things began to come together—or perhaps collide. At that time, the early 1970s, a type of parallel evolution had brought my two disparate focuses into alignment. In anthropology I was becoming aware of a new willingness among American anthropologists to use the perspective and methods developed in the study of exotic cultures to study aspects of their own culture. In one semester I read monographs on residents of the inner city and homeowners in a new planned development and a doctoral dissertation on the very "student ghetto" where I happened to be living at the time.

It was clear that the strategy of learning about a community by living in it, observing, and even participating in, a communal life, and then analyzing it in as broad a context as possible delivered results close to home that were as enlightening as in some distant archipelago.

At the same time, I was discovering that journalism was not the brutish enterprise I had feared. To my surprise, many of my colleagues at the student newspaper were more sensitive, more perceptive, and more honestly interested in the world than many of the students I had known, for example, in creative writing classes. There was a feeling among them that journalism was re-creating itself and that they were a part of that.

Our journalistic hero was not so much Bob Woodward (classic investigative reporter who coauthored *All the President's Men*) as it was Tom Wolfe. Wolfe led a widely divergent group of journalists into something that would come to be called new journalism. There was much produced that was excessive and superficial. Some of it was notable merely for the use of first-person narrative or the wild exuberance of the prose. But the best of it, the work that has held up over time, shares one characteristic: the writer penetrated the logic and customs of an exotic group and comprehended the world in the group's own terms.

When Wolfe showed us the LSD rituals of the Merry Pranksters in *The Electric Kool Aid Acid Test* or decoded the warrior society of fighter jocks in *The Right Stuff* or translated the exotic vocabularies of California surf rats in *The Pump House Gang*, he was doing so from inside the subculture with perceptions hard won through participant observation. Like any good field ethnologist, Wolfe brought to his work a wide cross-cultural reference and an eye for the interworkings of form and function.

So as I began my own journalistic work, it quickly dawned on me that the things I valued in anthropology were of tremendous value in reporting. That realization not only affected the way I went about collecting information but had tremendous bearing on the subjects I chose.

I was not as interested in covering student government politics as I was in probing the values and folkways of the leadership fraternity that brokered the election through the campus Greek system. It turned out that the currency of trade in this system were résumé plums, doled out by elected student officers to the fraternities that had proved alliance by delivering large blocks of votes.

Examining this phenomenon as an "anthro-journalist" or "media anthropologist" yielded a different kind of story from what would have been written by a traditional journalist. Instead of focusing on the scandal of brokered elections, we were interested in how the participants in the system perceived their roles, how they maintained their public morality or realigned it, and how the in-groups viewed the rest of the campus community.

This approach made it clear that the election brokering continued to exist because it fulfilled an important function in a community that was too transient, distracted, and apathetic to form an effective polity en masse. But an even more significant function, as we discovered, was the recruitment and training of the future leaders of state government. For three generations the young men (and until recently it was an all-male society) who came up through the closed, dynastic society of the leadership fraternity had gone on to fill the key law firms and political offices that dominated state government. (Of course, once the system was exposed, the antidemocratic values that dominated the fraternity groups raised enough outrage in the general student population that the brokerage system failed, new antipatronage laws were passed, and the campus political system evolved into something different from what it was.)

The idea that I was mixing anthropological inquiry with mass-audience journalism became explicit by the time I left the university and began working for metropolitan newspapers. My approach did not always fit comfortably in the culture of mainstream journalism. For one thing, my stories tended to be longer than editors were trained to accept, and the strategy of exploring a topic from the inside out could seem odd to those raised in a world of who, what, when, where, and why. In a profession obsessed with getting the story fast, these articles took weeks to prepare. The stories were revealing, but they were not traditional investigations. They were filled with what journalists call "color," but they were not ordinary feature stories.

Luckily for me, readers responded to the same things that made me respond to that introductory anthropology class years earlier. If we tend to fear or distrust those whose experience and outlook are different from our own, we are certain to be curious about them. There is something uniquely satisfying about catching a glimpse of the world through a very different set of eyes, through a very different reality filter. Among dozens of other stories that made extensive use of anthropological perspectives, I wrote what amounted to popularized monographs on a group of Florida Indians who, until the 1950s, had escaped all but minimal contact with European culture by living on islands in the Everglades; the descendants of a vanished hippie culture still living in a commune in 1980; a high school football team; a highly repressed, underground community of homosexuals living in Cincinnati; a community of small-acreage family farms in the Ohio valley; an urban underclass community in the ruins of a nineteenth-century German immigrant village; a group of highly educated people who believed in past-life regression and the writings of a psychiatrist turned new age prophet; and the naked dancers working in a run-down roadside bar.

My methodology differed from traditional journalism in some subtle, and some not-so-subtle, ways: I used question-answer interviews only when I could not get at the information I needed through direct observation of subjects in their normal environment. I used informants not so much as "sources" but, in the more anthropological sense, as intermediaries who could translate concepts in one culture/subculture into mainstream terms and ultimately introduce me to less "acculturated" individuals whose trust I would then work to gain. Instead of striving to understand people in terms of the cultural grid of a mainstream newspaper, I worked to understand the world through the categories and strategies of the subject. When researching background, I always look for ethnographic literature in addition to previous journalism on the topic.

But there are ways in which what I do is classic journalism and antithetical to anthropological research. Even when I work on something for a long time, it is measured in months, not years. I am interested in creating a dramatic narrative, not just concisely delivering data. When a university press decided to publish my work on the Florida Indian group with the aim of appealing to a popular audience, the academic review panel objected on the basis that it was written in a popular style.

Sixteen years into my newspaper career, I do not doubt that I am far more journalist than anthropologist. But I like to think that it is not quite as significant a distinction as it once was.

Chapter 6

The Anthropologist as Trade Book Author

Jack Weatherford

Stories about publishing have the predictability of stories about divorce. Everyone seems to have one, and nobody wants to hear it. Like the compulsion of the ancient mariner to wander the earth playing his sad story, something from deep inside the writer forces out repeated confessions of these it-was-hell-but-I-survived-it tales.

My sequence of sorrows usually begins with the printer who released my book with conflicting titles on the inside and outside, and from there I work up to the one about the publicist who issued a national press release about my book but had my name wrong. I lose interest in these dueling scars as soon as I am topped by another writer, such as the woman who appeared before a talk-show audience only to find out that the publisher had released someone else's book in her cover.

Writers love to show wounds much the same way that anthropologists show the ankle scars from the piranha, barbed wire scratches sustained while escaping the terrorists in the Sudan, or a limp resulting from a wild truck ride across Burma. Such merit badges of achievement inspire the uninitiated who hope to acquire similar stories for their captive audiences of undergraduate students.

Somewhere amid all those stories must be some rewards that

make fieldwork as valuable to an anthropologist as trade publication is to an author. Writing for a trade market offers a wonderful opportunity to reach new audiences, to be creative in new forms of expression, and to spread the fun and fascination of anthropology. It also offers another income in a milieu of declining academic salaries and reduced grant opportunities.

Articles on how to publish can be as daunting as looking at a manual on how to get a driver's license or reading the graduate catalog on how to get a doctorate. The steps quickly become obstacles, and the process seems depressingly long and totally illogical. Like most social processes, however, getting a trade book published is more easily done than explained, and it is difficult to generalize from one person's experiences.

Fortunately for potential trade writers, an agent, editor, and publicist can help ease you through the process. The more the writer knows about who these other people are and how their roles function in the publishing culture, the more useful they become to the writer. Fortunately, however, we need to know only *what* they do, and we do not need to know precisely *how* they do it.

One of the first things to note in entering the trade publication world is the division into different categories of books. The large, commercial publishers manufacture three types of products: text, trade, and mass-market books. Such publishers rarely handle academic books, which are more likely to be published by nonprofit and specialty presses.

If the academic text is a systematic survey across an unknown landscape, a trade book must be a well-defined path through it. The path may be winding or straight, narrow or wide, colorful or frightening, but it must be clearly demarcated since it is intended for people who do not normally tread on such ground. The trade book is for an audience that will read the book only once and not walk down that path again, in contrast to the academic book or textbook, which can serve as a resource to be consulted and examined repeatedly by people already knowledgeable about the area.

Although targeted for a general audience, the trade book should not be confused with a mass-market book. The trade books are the domain of serious nonfiction whereas mass-market books offer celebrity biographies, how-to books, new diets or exercise books, and recovery books. Mass markets often make their debut in paperback rather than cloth covers, and they sell in grocery stores, drugstores, and newspaper stands. Virtually all anthropological works published for profit and sold primarily in general-interest stores can be considered trade books rather than mass-market or academic books. By contrast most anthropological works sold through college bookstores would be textbooks or else academic books.

The author of a trade book plays the leading role in the writing of the book, but on the day the manuscript plops into the mailbox, the author is demoted to the role of a supporting player. Putting the manuscript in the mail is equivalent to watching one of your children graduate from school. You are entitled to feel proud, and you will forever have a vested interest, but you never again have the power over them that you once had.

Producing a book is always a collaborative effort in which the author plays a role at many crucial junctures, but the author is only one part of a group endeavor. After the work of the author, the manuscript falls under the control of an agent, an editor, and finally a publicist. No matter how good the original manuscript, it will not be a successful trade book without the hard work and collaboration of all members of the team.

THE AGENT AS GATEKEEPER AND MATCHMAKER

If you enjoy selling your own car for above the blue-book value by using classified ads and having an army of potential buyers tear up your lawn on the pilgrimage to your garage, if you spurn high-priced lawyers in favor of a do-it-yourself divorce kit available only through late-night cable television advertisements, if you enjoy assembling your own computer and computer table from wholesale parts available through army surplus catalogs, then you will enjoy selling your own manuscript to a publisher. Anyone else should find a literary agent.

Commercial publishers rarely buy books from writers; they buy them from agents. Most editors receive too many manuscripts to read, and they usually return unsolicited manuscripts unread and unopened.

The publishing industry depends on agents as the first line of defense against nuts, trash, and law cases. Agents control the gateways to trade publishing and make the initial selections of what has commercial potential. The agent targets the manuscript by knowing which publishers want which kinds of manuscripts, and within each house they know which editor at which imprint might like the book.

The agent rarely makes academic judgments on a manuscript or gives advice on writing it beyond whether or not it can be sold. During the first ten years that Lois Wallace represented me as literary agent she rejected three of my manuscripts and sold three as trade books. Of the three books she rejected she advised me to sell one to an academic market, and she told me to bury the other two. In rejecting half of my work, she was not passing an intellectual judgment on them; she was telling me only the commercial truth. The books may be works of genius, but they have no market.

Rather than saying that agents sell books, I should probably say that agents sell book ideas, and the coin of trade is the book proposal. After discussing an idea with an editor, the agent usually sends the editor a written proposal, which consists of a two-or three-page overview of the book, a detailed table of chapter contents, and one or two sample chapters. After reading the proposal, the editor may wish to see the entire manuscript, but most sales are made on the proposal itself.

It is important for academic authors to know that even when they have an entire manuscript, most publishers will need a proposal since that is what they discuss and pass around the table at staff meetings. For the first three books I published, I had to write a proposal in order to sell them, even though I had already written the entire manuscript.

Most agents charge a 15 percent commission on everything they sell; they get 15 percent of whatever the author gets. You should not pay an agent to evaluate a manuscript any more than you would pay a realtor to examine your house. Agents earn money by selling books, not by evaluating or editing them or by dispensing general advice to writers.

The agent's fee or commission should include virtually all operating costs of the agent. I sometimes talk with writers who pay their agents odd fees for photocopying manuscripts or even for long-distance telephone calls on the writer's behalf, but in my dealings with the Lois Wallace Agency, I have never been charged anything beyond the flat percentage.

The first step in a process is often the most difficult and the most crucial, and finding an agent is both of these. It takes time at the beginning, but it is not as daunting as the idea may seem.

The best way to get a literary agent is the same way you would find a real estate agent or a new dentist: you ask your friends and your friends' friends. Because agents usually have special areas of expertise, the best way to find the right agent for you is asking for a recommendation from someone whose work you like.

If you plan to publish for national distribution, it is best to use a New York agent since the trade book business centers on Manhattan. If you hope to write for a more specialized audience such as a regional one, you may wish to use an agent in that region.

If you do not know anyone with an agent, you can find the names of agents from directories available in the writing section of any general bookstore, from local writers' groups, or from the National Writer's Union, which is headquartered in New York but also has several regional offices and local chapters. Attending a single workshop with a local writing group can easily start you on the right track.

Once you find the agent, it is helpful to understand where the crucial decision points are for your book. Agents do not concentrate on royalty negotiations. The royalties for trade books follow a fairly standard formula. The author receives 10 percent of the cover price for the first 5,000 copies, 12.5 percent of the next 5,000, and 15 percent of all books sold after 10,000. This is always based on the cover (retail) price of the book. A book listed for $25 should produce $3.75 for the writer, even though some discount houses may sell the book for only $19.95. The royalties remain $3.75 until the publisher takes the book out of print and remainders the excess copies.

The commercial skill of agents comes into play first, by placing the book at the right house and second, by negotiating the largest advance they can. When agents sell a manuscript, they negotiate a price that is usually called the "advance," even though the author does not receive it all up front. The money comes in two installments, usually half at the time of signing the contract and half when the finished manuscript is accepted by the publisher. Thus on an "advance" of $30,000, the author receives only $15,000 at the signing of the contract, and it could be a year or more before the remainder is paid. Sometimes a different payment schedule may include several payments based on chapters completed; this usually depends on the financial needs and work habits of the author.

First-time authors can be so anxious to see their book in print that they pay less attention to the advance on the assumption that once published, the book will be good enough to sell on its own merit. The advance, however, indicates how much publishers are willing to invest in the book and is a good predictor of how much work they will devote to it and how well they will promote the book. A publisher who pays $2,000 for a manuscript has little incentive to promote it. A publisher who pays $100,000 for a manuscript has to promote it heavily to recover the initial investment. Thus, the greater the advance the agent can negotiate, then the greater the commitment from the publisher to promote the book.

A writer who is interested only in getting a book into print and is not interested in how many copies will be sold or how much money will be made should work with academic publishers or smaller nonprofit presses and not commercial publishers. For such a person to work with a commercial publisher would produce only irritation and disappointment on both sides.

The author's investment in a book is work—the work of researching, thinking, and writing the book; a publisher's primary investment is money. The advance should reflect the value of the author's work because in most cases that is the only money the author will ever receive for that book. Most commercial books never earn back their advances.

After selling the book, the agent sells secondary rights. The author can sell serial rights for excerpts of the manuscript to magazines or newspapers for publication anytime before the book's publication date. These secondary rights belong exclusively to the author until the publication date of the book, and such rights can produce nearly as much money as the book rights if sold to large magazines.

The sale of secondary rights is important not merely for the money it generates for the writer but because the sale alerts the publisher to other market interest in the work. The sale of secondary rights catches the interest of the publisher much more than any number of letters from friends about how important the book is and how often they will use it in a classroom. Publishers, like everyone else, like to be reassured by their peers. Having a magazine or newspaper editor buy a work offers warm reassurance to the book publisher that the author has produced a commercial product.

After publication the agent will try to sell foreign language rights or may be involved in television or film rights, but the main function of a literary agent is to sell books. Other agents may be needed for sales outside the book world.

With the signing of the contract, the main role of the agent has been fulfilled, and emphasis then passes to the editorial process.

EDITOR AS PRODUCER AND GODFATHER

The author is the writer of the book, but the editor is its producer. Like a good godfather, the editor makes problems disappear and attends to pesky details while freeing you to write. The editor oversees every step of the process, of which writing is only one small part. After the initial decision to acquire the manuscript, the primary work of the editor takes nine months starting from receipt of the final manuscript.

The stereotype of editors laboring over, and encouraging, the creative prose of their genius authors may never have been an accurate image, but it certainly does not pertain to today's publishing world. Editors have too many responsibilities overseeing the cover design, coordinating printing schedules, acquiring new properties, negotiating with agents, and dealing with lawyers to spend much effort on the writing of the book.

The writer of a trade book usually depends more on friends and professional colleagues than on the editor for hand-holding and long, penetrating discussions about the text. Yet, the editor is usually the only other person in the book production who really shares the writer's overall perspective and commitment to the book. In selecting your manuscript, the editor has taken a chance on you, and the editor's own position in the publishing house will be determined by the kinds of manuscript he or she selects.

The editorial work may consume less time than a writer might like, but the advice given is usually crucial. I find that my talk with editor James Wade, who bought three of my first five books, is usually at the "book level" or "chapter level," but rarely at the paragraph or sentence level. He gives me utterances such as:

> "We want the reader to get to the point here. Can you cut the first chapter in half?"
> "The middle of the book bogs down; bring in some examples."
> "Why do you spend so much time in chapter 3 on Columbus if you don't ever mention him again in the book?"
> "Why do readers care about potatoes? They may be very important to you, but you've got to make readers care if you want them to read this much about tubers."
> "Movies have previews, but books just tell the story."
> "Drop chapter 6; the whole world hates a smart ass."

Although such comments may be brief, they usually carry great importance because the editor is trying to read the book not as a friend of the author but as the producer of a commercial product.

Tim Foote, an editor at *Smithsonian*, is often quoted as saying "Everybody needs an editor," a comment he made after hearing that Hitler had first named his book *Mein Kampf: Four-and-a-Half Years of Struggle Against Lies, Stupidity, and Cowardice.* Today, however, much of the editing of manuscripts comes from assistant editors who supply detailed information at the chapter and paragraph level, pointing out poor transitions of theme or tangled knots of prose. A final editing with a line editor will bring your use of commas into agreement with the usual policy of the house.

Primary editors supervise all of these other editors, but their real importance comes not for what they do *to* the manuscript but what they do *for* it. If the book is to succeed, editors must build an internal coalition of support for it within the publishing house. They work to excite other people's interest in the commercial prospects for the book.

The Anthropologist as Trade Book Author

Occasionally the writer can help in this process, as by supplying slides for use in an editorial meeting, giving names of prominent "experts" who may offer good quotes, or in various other ways unique to each particular book. For the most part, however, this phase of the work continues without the writer's involvement or even knowledge, and like every political process it has a thousand nuances that one cannot understand without having been initiated into the culture, finances, and personalities of that particular publishing house.

I simply have to trust my editor.

Publishers usually release two or three lists of books a year, and for each list they have a sales conference in which the local sales representatives of that company gather to hear about the upcoming releases. The editor usually makes the pitch to them, and he or she can excite them by raising this book near the top of their interest list or can let them know that it is a good but minor work for special audiences.

The skilled editor knows how to build support in the sales force even before the meeting by "sharing" the manuscript with specially selected sales representatives who may help talk up the book at the meeting. In turn the sales representatives may "share" the manuscript of the page proofs with selected bookstore buyers who order in large quantities or have a respected position within their industry. All of this helps to bring more book people—sales representatives and booksellers—into the consensus that this book will be an important one when released.

The editor takes the manuscript to various book clubs, of which there are an increasing number. A book club deal requires a new contract with lower royalties, and the author divides the royalties with the publishing house. Despite the lower royalties, book clubs have high sales to well-targeted audiences. They make an important addition to the coalition of interests supporting the manuscript, and they are taken as a primary signal by the book publisher that the book will produce good sales.

Editors make the strategy to sell the paperback rights. Depending on the market, they may publish the paperback edition as well as the hardcover edition, or they may sell the paperback rights to another house. If they sell it, they must decide whether to do so before the publication date or wait until after the reviews and hardcover sales figures become known.

A sale to another house brings in another advance payment, which must be split between the author and the hardback publisher, and it is another sign of commitment by yet another segment of the publishing industry. Sale of paperback rights does not mean that the original publisher dislikes the book but merely that the publishing house wanted to make as much money on its financial investment as quickly as possible. Such a sale to another publisher also brings faster money to the author.

All of these factors together determine how many copies of the book the publisher will print. Publishers act conservatively. The average printing for a trade nonfiction book in the larger publishing houses is around 7,500 (much less for fiction).

If the publishers print too few, they can easily print more as needed, but if they publish too many, the publishers may be stuck with them. A large number of remaindered hardback books can also prevent sales of paperback, so a large, unsold printing hurts both publisher and author. Every author wants a large printing, but for both publisher and author, a small profit on a small printing helps more than a large loss on a large printing.

As publication day arrives, the editor steps back, and the spotlight falls on the publicist. This does not mean that the editor's work is finished, but the fate of the book has pretty much been determined at this point.

Conventional publishing wisdom used to maintain that a book had three months of shelf life in which to prove itself. If that was ever true, it is certainly no longer so. *Before* publication, a trade book must prove itself by acquiring a following of supporters from the editorial staff, the sales representatives, the buyers of paperback rights, book clubs, and the people who sell the list to the large bookstore chains and who place orders at local bookstores. On publication day a book must be vigorous and ready to take off, or it is declared dead and has only its author to support it and to seek as many sales as possible among family, friends, and colleagues.

PUBLICIST AS SHAMAN AND SNAKE CHARMER

Publicists talk too fast and leave me feeling socially and sartorially inadequate. I greatly admire them the same way that I admire those young New Guineans who jump off high platforms with only vines tied to their feet. Either their timing is perfect and the performance is breathtaking, or else it is total disaster.

Watching a publicist reduce six years of my best work and creative thought to ad copy provokes great anxiety. "The amazing story of how the potato conquered the world—From Timbuktu to Tibet—Explore the mysteries with a real-life Indiana Jones." They can reduce a whole life of research to a sequence of short and action-packed phrases that seem delicately poised between banality and genius. I particularly feel inadequate when the publicist explains better in one line what it took me a chapter to develop.

Despite all that, the publicists know how to bring your book to other people's attention. They get you far more readers than even the best of authors can find on their own.

The publicist comes into action very late in the publishing process and usually only if the bookstores order large quantities of the book before publication. In a sense publicity is not something that the publishers do for the author; they do it for the bookstores.

Bookstores order books prior to publication with the understanding that the publisher will allocate a certain amount of money to promoting it and perhaps on the condition that the author will promote the book in the particular town of that bookstore. This is in much the same way that a grocer who stocks a particular brand of toothpaste depends on the toothpaste manufacturer to advertise that brand of toothpaste. No one would expect a manufacturer to advertise a toothpaste that few stores stocked.

Publicity may rack up sales for movie star biographies, novels, and lurid exposés, but it rarely creates high sales for serious nonfiction books, which have much more specialized audiences. Authors sometimes hold out hope that their book will be catapulted to fame by a good review on the front page of the Sunday book supplement of the *New York Times*. The chances that an unknown book will be on the first page of the *Times* book supplement are less than 1 in 50,000.

Rather than trying to create publicity for nonfiction trade books, the publisher releases a list of such works and then sees which ones survive in the market. When Arbor House published my study of the red-light district of Washington, D.C., they simultaneously released the memoirs of Congressman Robert Bauman, who had lost office in a sex scandal, and the memoirs of Sidney Biddle Barrows, who had been arrested for running a house of prostitution and who became known as the "Mayflower Madam."

The congressman and I were left at the gate eating the dust that the Mayflower Madam generated as her sales took off. Naturally, Arbor House invested the money in further publicizing her book rather than mine.

I frequently hear complaints from some writers because their agents are not helping enough with publicity. The literary agent (who works for the author) is very different from the publicist or publicity agent who works for the publisher. Literary agents sell rights but rarely become directly involved in the publicity campaigns.

The relationship between the author and publicist is short but very intense. A few months before publication date, the publicist will gather biographical information and together with the editorial staff develop a strategy for marketing the book. The strategies are as varied as the kinds of books and of publicists and authors working together.

Publicists place articles in newspapers and magazines, and they book interviews for radio and television. They do not usually organize lecture tours to colleges, museums, or civic groups. For such special activities a writer/lecturer needs a booking agent who works similarly to a literary agent.

Publicists rarely promote sales within a particular discipline such as anthropology. Most publishers have educational divisions that handle sales for the educational market. The publicist is concerned primarily with immediate sales between the time a book appears on the market and the next list appears. The publicist is primarily concerned with potential sales to a college a year or two from publication date.

A good publicist can help a trade writer reach new audiences and find new markets outside the academic and education arena. Through their work with the news media, the publicists also expand the impact of the writer's ideas to audiences who will not read the book. In this regard publicists are purveyors of your ideas as well as your books.

The troika of agent, editor, and publicist, together with the unseen staff of professionals who work with them, can remove the drudgery from writing. When working closely together and coordinated through the author, they can bring in financial rewards as well as give the writer the chance to do what most writers enjoy the most —to think and read and write.

Chapter 7

The Anthropologist as Television Subject

Helen Fisher

"Miracles sometimes occur, but one has to work terribly hard for them," it has been said. That is television. You can work six weeks to design a perfect seven-minute segment. Even then, the interviewer, the cameramen, the audience, and you have to act with symphonic coordination for any true magic to occur. That is why I am always nervous in the waiting room, universally known in television as the "green room."

How to overcome my fear I would like to know. It is difficult enough to present a complicated topic simply, clearly, and accurately, but sweating palms and a racing heart make it much, much harder. I have tried meditating by concentrating on a shiny doorknob and breathing evenly, but it has not worked. Sometimes I press my palms against a wall, a technique I once read Yul Brynner practiced. Actually it helps. But nothing cures stage fright—except perhaps the stage itself. Because I want to be invited back to many of these television programs, each appearance is a performance. I have discovered only one antidote to panic—I am prepared.

By the time I am in the green room I know exactly what I want to say and how I want to say it. If the interview is a four-minute segment on NBC's "The Today Show," for example, I have established four or five points I want to make, the direction of the conversation, and the finale. Days before the interview a producer has approved these too. Then the producer writes Jane Pauley's crib sheet while I write mine.

I design these notes carefully, isolating each point on a separate sheet of typing paper. I write key words and phrases very large in pencil, then ink over them in red, blue, green, or brown Magic Marker. I underline one-liners four or five times in black. Some words stand an inch tall; I write others sideways or otherwise askew. All sorts of ancillary remarks I write in the margins. Then to accentuate specific thoughts I surround my various ideas in inky hearts, diamonds, or other designs that act as cues.

With important words in huge handwritten letters and with arrows, hearts, and squiggles to accentuate my extra points, each sheet of paper takes on a distinct personality. I then use these pages as mnemonics. If the interviewer goes off on a tangent, I can recall the total visual image of my crib sheet in an instant, then mine the margins for an appropriate response. But these outlandish-looking notes have other purposes as well. As I design a sheet of paper I am memorizing what I want to say, picking the perfect word or phrase, ordering my ideas. This way what often looks like a spontaneous remark is actually totally planned. Last, these cue cards serve as faithful friends. I take them into the green room and consult them as I fret.

Next in the odyssey is makeup. From the green room the guest is directed into the makeup room, where we confer about eyes and lips and hair. I generally lose these discussions. Television people like lipstick on their guests, something I never wear, but I always give in. I also defer to tradition in my dress. Cameramen do not like you to wear white or black; they say these colors make the camera jump. They do not like busy patterns either. So I always wear a solid-colored silk shirt and earrings that do not shine. I almost never wear a suit—for a different reason. By the time a viewer sees an academic on television, they are already impressed with your credentials. They are fairly well convinced you are obtuse, aloof, and stuffy. I hope to convey that anthropology is useful—and entertaining. So I try not to look "tweedy" or too businesslike.

Back in the green room I continue my effort to relax. Often I watch the in-house television monitor that broadcasts the show. This can be important. If an incident occurs on one of the segments before mine, perhaps I will play on it during my interview. A casual conversation with another guest is good, too; it warms me up. But I prefer to sit and stare. Above all, I stay out of the way. Producers and other staff mill about. Guests often joke or preen. I find the energy unnerving. So I isolate. When I am next, they will find me; I am sure of that.

When the time comes, a producer ushers you onto the set; it is always a big, cold room with cameras the size of Volkswagens and lots of very busy people wearing antennae on their heads. As a member of the camera crew helps me weave the microphone through my blouse, I study the cameras, the television monitors, the audience if there is one, the producers, and the host. Then when my interviewer comes to sit beside me, I instantly try to get to know him or her. Does she like anthropology? If we are going to talk about divorce or some aspect of love relationships (which is my specialty), I need to know if she is married. Is she going through a divorce? Does she have children? What parts of this conversation are important to her life?

In moments we are on the air. I listen carefully to the question, which is often not what I expected. As things get going, we set a pace, normally a fast one, and keep at it. If she is skilled, she will interrupt me continually; interviewers do not like a monologue. They cannot tolerate a silence—"dead air." Despite all my preparation the interview almost never goes as I had planned. Hosts have their own agenda. Unless I take the lead—which is not polite—the conversation can move into unknown territory fast. When I do not know an answer, I say so; then I try to turn the question into something that brings the conversation back on track. I always use my hands. I normally lean forward. I try to modulate my voice. I keep my answers relatively short. Sometimes I interrupt. When appropriate, I smile.

Smiling is effective. On a television show in Pittsburgh, the senior producer once rushed onto the set, saying, "I am going to use your segment to show doctors how to perform on TV." "Why?" I asked, wondering what I had said that had struck him as intelligent. He replied, "Because you smiled." American academics think that to be believed they must be grim. I have seen more than one perfectly affable scientist in the green room turn into a stern, rigid, pompous person on the set. It's a mistake. Viewers already think you are important; you are on television. Your job is to be human, to make your message interesting, and if your topic warrants it, to make it entertaining too. An excellent way to personalize your topic is with an occasional smile.

After the interview comes my most important moment. As the producer rushes me to the lobby or back into the green room, I make my pitch: "You know, anthropology can lend perspective to almost any issue, from child abuse, to working mothers, to why people give gifts, to how they lie. If you ever need a fresh view on any topic, please call. I know a lot of anthropologists, and I am happy to give you a lead any time." Then I hand out my card and vanish.

There are different kinds of television shows. Each has special traps, specific opportunities. The four-minute segment in a national show, such as "The Today Show," has the virtue of being one-on-one. When I had a contract with NBC in 1984-1985, I picked the topic, then talked with Jane Pauley by myself. The solo performance is good because you have some control over what goes on. But this four-minute time slot can be brutal; four minutes is not much time—not enough to overcome your nervousness, yet plenty of time to say something very foolish.

Talk shows like "Geraldo" have different problems. You are on with several other guests, and Geraldo rules. You have to be forceful if you want to break in on the conversation because you do not share the camera; it is on one guest or another. As a result you have to talk over another party to win center stage. Some guests are exceedingly aggressive and very good at interrupting one another. I can do it, and I have. But I think it is often more effective to sit tight and wait my turn.

On these group-interview shows, generally one of the guests wants to attack me; that is the way these shows are often designed. So either they do not believe in evolution, they cannot tolerate a scientific discussion about divorce, infatuation, or adultery, or something else irks them, and they lunge, verbally. In this situation I generally let them rage; then I make my point. This is easier said than done, however, and sometimes I join the verbal melee. But the audience loves an underdog, and television is a blatant medium. So I try to use the camera and look disgusted instead. The visual image can be so much more powerful than words.

The street interview, like the kind we get at anthropology conventions, has its own set of rules. Producers hope you will talk in "sound bites"—concise, entertaining miniparagraphs. They cannot abide a windbag. But film editors can use terse sentences either as they are delivered or separately if the segment needs to be rearranged. The trick is to be brief, be friendly, and make your statements relevant and clear—no jargon.

What, then, are the problems of presenting anthropological concepts and data on television? Foremost, anthropology is not a precise science. We admire complex, wordy, convoluted arguments. To many anthropologists simplicity implies reductionism. But complicated arguments rarely make good television. Instead one has to distill an argument to its essence. No caveats. No discussion of the problems with the data. No time to dissect the subtleties or the nuances of the idea. You have to make up your mind exactly what you wish to say and say it—boldly. This can be painful. Equally distressing, anthropologists are trained to quote one another's work. On television you simply cannot drop all these names.

But there are much thornier problems than being brief and not citing sources. Anthropology is a science about people. In my television appearances I talk about evolution, animal behavior, human sexuality, our emotions, and social customs around the world. On one occasion my segment created havoc; it was on "The Today Show." I was talking about etiquette, and I mentioned that the Chinese were reluctant to say no when asked to do a favor. That afternoon a national organization of Chinese Americans called the senior producer of the program and demanded "equal time" to present their point of view. I had not slandered anyone; I had not even mentioned Chinese Americans. But this activist group saw my discussion as an opportunity to lobby. They did not get equal time, but the acrimony made me look bad. Our science can stir up feelings and galvanize private interest groups when one least expects them.

Another intrinsic problem with doing anthropology on television stems from a basic tenet of our academic training: we are taught to be participant-observers, not activists. We do not get involved. This led me to another difficult moment on a national television show, an afternoon entertainment show in Los Angeles. During the first segment I gave my theory for the evolution of infatuation, attachment, and desertion. The host and audience seemed fascinated. After the commercial break the interviewer launched into an unexpected conversation, the practical matter of how to preserve relationships. He wanted me to give a prescription on how to save your marriage. I replied I was not a trained psychologist; I did not wish to give advice. The host was horrified. After the show the senior producer emerged to show me to the door; her face was purple. How dare I raise such provocative facts about American family life and offer no solutions? I was stunned.

That evening changed my life. I was visiting a friend and colleague, anthropologist Barbara Pillsbury, at her home in Malibu, and over dinner I recounted this event. She fell silent. Then she remarked, "Margaret Mead would have given the audience some advice."

From this experience I learned perhaps the single most important rule of television. Behind ivy-covered walls scientists are allowed to deliver data without tying it to America today. Not so on television; this is the "real world." No host, no producer, no audience wants to hear from anthropologists unless we take into account American issues and use our data to address these problems. So many times I see a colleague working on an intellectual problem that appears irrelevant; with just a little twist, he or she could make it applicable instead. Today when a television host asks me how to save a marriage, I am prepared. I have read the literature on divorce, and after reminding the audience that I am not a psychologist, I report on what therapists and counselors say.

Is it ethical to give marital advice without training in this field? Is it ethical to simplify a complex topic? Is it ethical to recount someone else's ideas and not cite the author or to tell stories about another culture out of context? Yes, I think it is. But you have to be very careful with your words. That is why I write out my crib sheets, mnemonics that look like e. e. cummings and Kandinsky rolled into one, and why my palms sweat as I push them against the green room wall. Television is dangerous. Even one minute of air time is enough to make a bad mistake. But television is also the single most effective way to broadcast anthropological data and ideas. I think it is unethical not to take this chance.

These, then, are the realities of television work. What are the myths? Perhaps the biggest myth has to do with money. I rarely get paid for an appearance. When you are selling a book, you never get paid; producers feel they are doing you a favor, which they are. After my book, *The Sex Contract: The Evolution of Human Behavior*, had been in print for more than two years, I began to resent my unpaid performances, however. So I joined AFTRA, the American Federation of Television and Radio Artists. Now that I am a dues-paying union member, television producers must give me a minimum wage for talk shows, a fee of about $87 (net) for a local show, about $350 (net) for a national appearance. But getting this money is difficult; you have to ask. Once you have raised the issue, you have to be prepared to lose the job; I have lost several. Because there are a lot of scientists who are willing to go on television for no pay (and I am often one of them), producers just get someone else.

Another myth is that the interviewer has a "point of view." I have never found this to be true. The hosts I have worked with are paid professionals; not one has ever promoted his or her ideas. They have no investment in your response either. No one expects you to pander to public fads or tell the audience what it wants to hear. All the producers and the interviewer hope is that you will be original, spontaneous, interesting, clear, concise, provocative, and factually correct. What you say is up to you.

What you say is actually semiplanned, however. Long before the green room, the makeup, or the microphone, you and a producer from the show have developed the script together. This occurs during the preinterview—the most crucial part of being a subject on television. When a program is interested in your ideas, someone calls. It is always a producer, normally a woman. She introduces herself, tells you about the show, and begins to question you about your research. Now you are obliged to be smart and quick. You have no cue cards. While you talk, she listens, making up her mind.

Are you a monotone? Do you orate? Are you earnest, bright? Do you have something new to say? How much jargon do you use? Can you be flexible? Are you concise and pithy? If the producer likes what you say and how you say it, she will begin to isolate specific points. Then together you work up a script—the points to be covered and the direction the conversation ought to take. These she will write up and hand over to the host. Then the producer establishes the day and other logistics for the interview. But you are only as good as your last performance. There is no such thing as tenure in this vastly fickle field.

People have asked me how to get on television. The only way I know of is the way I did it: I wrote a book, and in the book I applied some of my ideas to America today. Publishing companies are eager to sell books, so if an author is willing, the publicity department attempts to get him or her on television. The trick, of course, is to do well enough to be asked back. This was my good fortune on "The Today Show." Someone had heard of me and told someone else, who called to invite me to make some comments on the subject of spring fever. After that performance I was asked to do a two-part segment on divorce. This double segment led to my contract with "The Today Show" in 1984-1985 and to appearances on other shows since then.

My segments vary widely in content. The "Four-Year Itch"—the kernel of my new data on divorce—is a common theme. But I have also designed programs such as "Evolution of Humor," "The Natural History of Lying," "The Anthropology of Eating," "Gift Giving Around the World," "Why Lip Surgery?," "Human Gestures," "Flirting," "The Marriage Squeeze," and programs on an assortment of other topics. This television work seems to continue by word of mouth; I have no agent. Producers call to ask if I can contribute an idea to some event in the news, or they call when they are building a program around some aspect of romance. Each time a new producer calls, I begin the same routine—auditioning during the preinterview, preparing the script with the producer, writing out my crib sheet, then walking into the green room in my silk, solid-colored shirt gripping my mnemonics until I am on the air.

My anthropological training has helped this process in several ways. During graduate school I learned to think on my feet. I also absorbed the essential skill of any social scientist, to research widely on my own. Speaking and writing clearly, however, were different matters. I took a night course after graduate school called How to Write. Speaking clearly—well, I practice this. But the most important thing my graduate training gave me was the "four-field" approach. Anthropology is a magnificent conglomerate of subdisciplines with a unique perspective on the world. "A way of seeing," Mead called it. Moreover, this rich, broad, multidisciplinary database focuses on nature's most interesting creature—humankind, ourselves.

Sometimes I am astonished at how we have kept our science so obscure. Television can change this.

Chapter 8

The Anthropologist as Television Journalist

James Lett

The world discovered television more than a generation ago, but anthropologists are just beginning to appreciate the profound cultural significance of the medium. Despite the fact that television is rapidly becoming ubiquitous in the world, already reaching "the largest and most heterogeneous audience of any form of communication in human history" (Rosten 1971, 137), and despite the fact that television, especially in industrialized societies, is increasingly responsible for defining public issues and shaping public opinion (Hood 1987), anthropologists have traditionally dismissed television as a trivial element of popular culture unworthy of serious attention. Informally, at least, anthropologists have tended to regard television as shallow and superficial (which it often is) and uninteresting and unimportant (which it definitely is not). All of that, fortunately, is changing. Conrad Kottak (1990, 9), in a recent comparative study of television in the United States and Brazil, observes that television's "effects are comparable to those of humanity's most powerful traditional institutions—family, church, state, and education." The significance of television as an agent of enculturation, as a source of information, and as a means of cultural homogenization is now unquestioned and may eventually prove to be unrivaled.

My principal interest, however, lies not with television as a whole but with a particular aspect of the medium, namely, television journalism. It is apparent to even a casual observer that television journalism plays a highly influential role in contemporary industrialized societies such as the United States. Television has been the average American's preferred source of news for more than three decades, which means simply that most adult Americans today obtain most of their information about events in the world from television newscasts. This should be especially important to anthropologists, who make their careers producing and analyzing information about events in the world, assuming anthropologists have an interest in sharing their information with a broad audience. In fact, some anthropologists have recognized the potential significance of television news for disseminating anthropological information. In a pioneering contribution to media anthropology, Eiselein and Topper (1976, 158) cogently observed that "the greatest opportunity for anthropological involvement in the broadcast media is in the area of news."

Anthropologists can become involved in television news as either *newsmakers* or *newscasters* (that is, as either the subjects of news reports or the producers of those reports), and the overwhelming majority of anthropologists, obviously, will prefer to be newsmakers rather than newscasters if they choose to have anything to do with television news. Elsewhere (Lett 1987a), I have urged *all* anthropologists to become involved in television news as newsmakers, and I have offered advice on what seem to me to be the best ways to accomplish that goal (Lett 1987b). (In chapter 7, Helen Fisher offers an excellent description of what anthropologists can expect as television newsmakers on live interview programs at the network level.) I know of no anthropologists, however, who have followed Eiselein and Topper's suggestion to become involved in television news as newscasters—other than myself.

From 1983 to 1986, after I earned my doctorate in cultural anthropology from the University of Florida, I spent three years working as a television journalist. As far as I know, I am the only professional anthropologist who has ever worked as a full-time television newscaster. I know of several anthropologists who work in various aspects of television (e.g., as documentary producers or advertising executives), and I know of anthropologists who work as full-time print journalists, but I do not know of any anthropologists who work in television as news reporters, producers, or anchors. To my knowledge my experience in television news is unique; I know for certain that it is rare, and I do not think it is probable that will ever change. Television journalism is not likely to become a career option for anything other than a small minority of anthropologists.

For anthropologists who possess a particular combination of interests, skills, and talents, however, I think television journalism can be a legitimate and viable career alternative. What I want to do here, then, is address myself to those anthropologists who are interested in considering the field of television journalism. If you are such an anthropologist, my experiences may give you some idea of what you can expect from television news.

First, you should be aware of the personal qualities you will need to succeed as a television journalist. Good oral and written communication skills top the list. The ability to work well and quickly under deadline pressure would be a close second. An eclectic range of interests is essential for most television journalists, and so too is a high tolerance for stress and frustration. Television journalists, much more so than print or radio journalists, must deal with the rewards and punishments of personal notoriety; you will have to accustom yourself to receiving unsolicited adoration and ire from strangers in public, both of which will usually be undeserved.

If you have these qualities, however, and if you would like to reach a substantially larger audience than most anthropologists ever reach, then television journalism deserves your serious consideration. As I have observed before (Lett 1986), cultural anthropology and television journalism share several fundamental similarities. Both professions are concerned with observing, recording, describing, and explaining human behavior. There are differences, important ones, in the assumptions, methods, and goals of the two disciplines, but anthropology and journalism have enough in common to be compatible. To achieve that compatibility, of course, requires compromise. For the anthropologist who chooses to work in television journalism, the challenge is to make journalism more anthropological (more holistic, more comparative, and less ethnocentric) and at the same time to make anthropology more journalistic (more accessible, more relevant, and less esoteric). What follows is the story of my attempts to do just that.

My first job in television was a part-time, unpaid position as the host and producer of a weeky half-hour public affairs interview program on the public access channel of the local cable television company in Gainesville, Florida. That was in September 1982, and I was nearing completion of my graduate study in anthropology. I had just begun to write my dissertation, having completed my course work and research for my doctorate, and I was beginning to think seriously about a job and making a living and other similarly unpleasant issues that I had managed until that point to avoid. At the time, I had decided on a career in applied anthropology, and the idea of media anthropology was especially appealing to me. The public access channel that the local cable television company made available presented an affordable and attainable opportunity for acquiring initial experience in television. (Such opportunities are still commonly available at most cable television companies around the country.)

The program, which was called "Cable Talk," was on the air for nine months. As host and producer, I had complete control of the program, both in front of the camera and behind it. Each segment of the program was devoted to a single controversial social issue, such as abortion, gun control, the equal rights amendment, gay liberation, and the teaching of creationism in public schools. Most shows featured a pair of guests who had been chosen because they could be counted on to take opposite sides of the issue at hand (there are always 2 sides to every issue in the world of television journalism, never 11 or 12 sides as there are in the real world). As host, I took an active role in questioning both guests, pointing out the illogic of their arguments when I perceived it (as I often did) and using my anthropological training to challenge their premises with comparative data. The program was taped in a single 30-minute segment and then broadcast unedited as though it were live.

"Cable Talk" was informative and timely and chock-full of anthropological data (as producer, I carefully researched each topic in advance and prepared an extensive list of notes that, as host, I held in my lap while we were taping). There was just one problem with the program: it was deadly dull. The answers my guests gave were typically long-winded, repetitive, and esoteric (I chose many of them from the large and readily available pool of academicians at the University of Florida), and the questions I asked were typically verbose, stilted, and multifaceted. I believed at the time that my anthropological training had prepared me for successful interviewing, and on one level I was correct: the interviews I conducted on "Cable Talk" did produce some interesting data.

On another level, however, I was very much mistaken. The success of an anthropological interview is measured primarily by the quality of the product (were useful data obtained?) and secondarily by the quality of the process (was rapport maintained?), while the success of a television interview is measured primarily by the quality of the process (was it an interesting and entertaining conversation for other people to listen to?) and only secondarily by the quality of the product (was the exchange informative?). Later I mastered some of the craft of live interviewing and learned how to make the interview flow, how to make it sound conversational, how to make myself and the subject comfortable in front of the camera, and how to retain the viewer's interest, but I did not know how to do any of those things when I hosted "Cable Talk," and as a result I cannot watch those tapes today without cringing.

Nevertheless, "Cable Talk" taught me some important lessons. It taught me, first, that television could be fun. There is an opening-night excitement to live television. Some people, depending on their temperament, are made uncomfortable by it; others thrive on it. I discovered that I enjoyed it. I learned, too, something about the power of the medium to reach and move members of the general public. Strangers would occasionally stop me in the grocery store to comment on a program, and none of the graduate student papers I had presented at scholarly conferences had ever received that kind of attention. The degree of exposure that could be gained from the local cable company's public access channel convinced me that the potential impact of *real* television could be enormous. Perhaps most importantly, "Cable Talk" taught me that I had a good deal more to learn about television and that I was going to have to acquire some expertise in broadcasting if I hoped to find work as a television journalist.

Fortunately, the University of Florida offered a wide range of opportunities for training in broadcast journalism. (This is likely to be true at any large university.) The College of Journalism and Communications at the University of Florida operated three radio stations and one television station when I was there in the early 1980s, and all of the stations offered local news programming. Those programs were produced in newsrooms staffed almost entirely by students (with the exception, in each case, of the news director, who was a member of the faculty), and the newscasts were delivered by students. (Again, this is a common situation at most large universities.) The student positions in each newsroom were ostensibly open only to undergraduate and graduate majors in broadcast journalism, but the high turnover rate and the fluctuations in the academic calendar frequently left the stations in need of temporary volunteer labor.

My next job in broadcasting was thus as a fill-in newswriter and newscaster at one of the radio stations during the three-week Christmas break. It was an opportunity to begin to learn some important skills: how to write for the ear as opposed to the eye, how to deliver a newscast, how to edit audiotape, how to recognize what journalists define as newsworthy, how to estimate the length of time required to read a given piece of copy, how to deal with the unexpected in a live newscast, how to conduct and record a telephone interview, and how to do a hundred other things that make up the routine of work in a radio newsroom. It was also an opportunity to make myself known to the Broadcasting Department, and that would soon pay a dividend in the form of expanded opportunities for experience. As a graduate student in anthropology, I was beginning to build a broadcasting résumé. For aspiring television newscasters, the importance of that cannot be overemphasized. There are no formal standards of certification or licensing in the journalism profession, which means that your claim to journalistic credentials will rest solely on your résumé. Anyone who works as a journalist is a journalist; anyone who does not, is not.

I took only one formal course in broadcasting at the University of Florida while I was building my television resumé: an upper-division undergraduate course in Television Reporting. The course was taught by the news director of WUFT-TV, the Public Broadcasting Service (PBS) affiliate television station operated by the university, and the students enrolled in the course provided the reporting staff for the half-hour local newscast broadcast Monday through Friday at 5:30 P.M. Other, more experienced students produced and anchored the program. (Once again, similar opportunities can be found at most major universities.) The course was generally open only to students majoring in broadcasting, but with my background in television, minimal though it was, I was able to get the instructor's permission to enroll.

In that one semester I learned the basics of television newscasting: how to operate a video camera, how to edit videotape, how to shoot "stand-ups" and "reversals," how to choose "bites," how to lay an audio track, how to write to available video—in short, I learned how to put a "package" together. (A "package"—also called an "SOT," for sound on tape—is a self-contained, edited news report, typically 90 seconds long, featuring the reporter's voice-over video narration, one or more recorded quotes from interviewees, cover video shot in the field, and, usually, a brief on-camera appearance by the reporter taped at the scene of the story.) The packages that I produced during that semester were unpolished and rudimentary, but they were adequate and demonstrated minimal competence. I saved the best half-dozen of them for my "resumé tape" (also called an "audition tape"—the first thing a prospective employer is going to want to see from any applicant for a job in television journalism), and that resumé tape was sufficient, three months later, to get me an entry-level job as a television reporter at a medium-sized station in south Florida. My experience was not atypical. The skills that are required to become employable in television journalism can be easily and quickly acquired.

In the three months between June 1983, when I completed my first course in television reporting, and September of that year, when I accepted my first full-time paid job in television journalism, I held two additional volunteer positions at the university station. That summer, I served one six-week stint as the producer of the daily newscast (the producer, in television news, is the person responsible for the content, order, and timing of the stories in the newscast), and one six-week stint as the news anchor. Thus, in the space of one year—a year during which I was writing my dissertation—I was able, on a part-time basis, to acquire all the experience and credentials I needed to work in television. The way I did it, of course, is not the only way to do it, but the point is that it can be readily accomplished.

For the next three years, I worked at WTVX-TV, a CBS affiliate station in Ft. Pierce, Florida, first as a reporter and then as an anchor-producer. Ft. Pierce is part of the "Market" that includes the city of West Palm Beach. There are approximately 200 television markets in the United States, ranked according to their population size (New York is the #1 market, Los Angeles is #2, Chicago is #3, and so on). Your chances of securing an entry-level position as a reporter, producer, or anchor are inversely proportional to the market's size: the higher the market's ranking, the lower your chances of being hired without extensive experience and/or outstanding ability. The West Palm Beach market is ranked in the 50s, and it is unlikely that stations in higher markets will hire beginning newscasters for on-air positions. In other words, if you want to be on the air, you should plan to start in a smaller city. Television journalism is a highly mobile profession, and upwardly mobile newscasters expect to change jobs every year or two, ideally moving each time to a station in a higher market.

During the first two years that I worked at WTVX, I was a general assignment reporter, which meant that I covered any and all stories that the producer and news director deemed newsworthy. Often, those stories centered on local government and local crime and had to be produced under extreme deadline pressure. As a result, I was often frustrated at my inability to introduce an anthropological context to such stories. Journalists have a fairly peculiar idea of what is and is not "news" (Lett 1987a: 357), and producers can be very resistant to story proposals that fall outside their standard set of assumptions.

There were many times, however, when I was able to incorporate an anthropological perspective in my reporting, and those instances were very satisfying. The area of south Florida that I covered was, and is, experiencing rapid urbanization and population growth, and individual citizens and local governments are being forced to deal with a wide range of cultural and environmental changes. As an anthropologist, I was able to appreciate the broader context of the interaction between the culture and the environment, and I tried to frame my stories in terms of that context. I never used terms like "acculturation" or "cultural ecology" or "cultural evolution" in my news reports, of course, but I made comparisons and drew parallels that referred implicitly to many such anthropological concepts.

It was frequently easier to incorporate an anthropological perspective in "feature" stories (that is, stories that dealt with human interest rather than "hard" news or "breaking" news), and for that reason I looked forward to doing features whenever possible. The outstanding example in my memory was a story I covered involving a group of local high school students who were making a three-week exchange trip to France. Against all standards of reasonable news judgment and sound fiscal management, my news director was persuaded to send me to Paris to cover the final week of the students' stay in France. Accompanied by a videographer, I followed a dozen impressionable American students from the Eiffel Tower to the Louvre to Notre Dame to the Folies Bergere, asking penetrating interview questions about culture shock and worldview and proxemics and phonology. When I returned, I produced a five-part series of reports that resembled nothing so much as a colorful introduction to cultural anthropology. The series won an Honorable Mention Award of Excellence from the National Education Association, but it ranks much higher than that in my estimation: reporting the story was wonderful fun.

During the last year that I worked at WTVX, I was promoted to anchor-producer of the daily half-hour noon newscast. As producer, I was solely responsible for the content and format of the program. One of the first things I did was to incorporate a live interview segment in the final ten minutes of the show. I was now able to resurrect what I had found most satisfying about "Cable Talk"—the ability to offer intelligent and informed discussion of significant social issues—but by this stage I was much more skillful at it, and I had a much larger audience. Even though I never used the word "anthropology" in those interviews, I enjoyed abundant opportunity to apply my anthropological knowledge. That experience convinced me that it was possible to combine anthropology and the media in a meaningful and satisfying way, and if I had not chosen to leave journalism for personal reasons (there were other interests I wanted to pursue and other opportunities that I wanted to take advantage of), I would still be happily producing and hosting a live news interview program today.

For anthropologists considering a career in television journalism, there are several explicit lessons to be derived from my experience. To begin, you should recognize and accept the fact that your anthropological credentials will mean nothing in the world of television journalism; in fact, a graduate degree in anthropology may well be regarded as more of a liability than an asset by your journalistic colleagues. Prospective employers will not care that you possess a special understanding of the human condition; they will care only that you can report, produce, or anchor a news story. When I was being interviewed for my first professional job in television, the news director asked me if I thought a person with a Ph.D. would be able to explain the news of the day to "Joe Six-Pack" (broadcasting's version of John Q. Public). In order to work as a journalist, I had to market myself as a journalist, and I generally kept my anthropological background and agenda to myself. This, after all, is a simple ethnographic truism: to be accepted as a member of a culture, you must talk and dress and act like a member of that culture.

In addition, you should be aware of the fact that a degree in journalism or broadcasting is neither necessary nor sufficient for employment as a television journalist. For that reason, I would *not* recommend pursuing a dual major or dual degrees in anthropology and journalism, unless you are in the early stages of your undergraduate career. I would certainly recommend that you take advantage of the opportunities for practical experience available in most broadcasting departments, but I frankly think that a degree in broadcasting would be more trouble than it is worth for someone who already has a degree in anthropology. You need the broadcasting skills, not the degree, and you can acquire the necessary skills by using the anthropological technique of participant observation. A résumé of practical experience in broadcasting will be more impressive to most news directors than a degree in broadcasting, and an applicant with a résumé is more likely to be granted a job interview than an applicant with only a degree to offer. In any event, the only thing that will get you an on-air job is the set of skills you demonstrate on your résumé tape.

Implicit in what I have been saying is the fact that television journalism calls for a particular set of talents and skills, and those are not necessarily the same talents and skills called for in anthropology. While intelligence and knowledge may be necessary traits for success in anthropology, for instance, there are some jobs in television journalism—such as anchor—where those attributes are not essential for success. Finding the job in television journalism for which you are best suited is a process of experimentation. I discovered, for example, that I was merely competent as a reporter and unexceptional as an anchor, but that I had a predilection for live interviewing. I did not realize that when I began my career in broadcasting—in fact, I mistakenly thought that I would be best suited for anchoring—and I had to go through a period of trial and error before I discovered where my true broadcasting talents lay. I suspect that most anthropologists would find themselves best suited for work behind the camera. The job of producer, for example, can directly utilize the anthropological penchant for holism, integration, and contextualization.

Yet another lesson to be gleaned from all this concerns the level of frustration you can expect to encounter as an anthropologist working in journalism. Anthropologists are accustomed to the luxury of lengthy research, painstaking analysis, and distant deadlines; journalists, of course, are accustomed to cursory research, instant analysis, and immediate deadlines. As an anthropologist, therefore, you will frequently find yourself wanting more time to do more research to provide more context for the news you are reporting, but as a journalist you will very rarely have the opportunity to follow those anthropological inclinations. Moreover, anthropological and journalistic standards of data collection can sometimes come into serious conflict. As an example—one I have offered elsewhere in more detail (Lett 1986: 35)—anthropologists and journalists have distinctly different notions about the nature of "objectivity." For scientific anthropologists, objectivity means being fair to the truth; for television journalists, objectivity means being fair to everyone involved. It can be very uncomfortable to be asked by a news director—as I have been—to deny or ignore the truth of the matter at hand in the interests of being "fair" to the people involved in the story (e.g., to report that evolution is "just a theory" as a means of being fair to creationists and others whose religious convictions do not allow them to accept the fact of evolution).

There are other practical considerations that I have not mentioned. It is widely unappreciated that there is a two-tier pay scale in television journalism. Those at the top (e.g., anchors in major markets) earn salaries comparable to those of professional athletes. Those at the bottom, however—and they constitute the majority of television journalists—earn salaries comparable to those of grade school teachers. There is another well-kept secret about television journalism: being a television newscaster is popularly perceived as glamorous and exciting, and, indeed, at times it can be, but it can also be very, very boring. For every hour I spent on the Champs Élysées shooting stand-ups with the Arc de Triomphe in the background, I spent ten hours on a metal folding chair in a crowded and unventilated auditorium listening to local politicians debate the merits of a proclamation to honor National Widgets Manufacturers' Month.

There are still other drawbacks. If you decide on a career as a television journalist, you will have to get used to working on holidays and to being on call for stories that break on nights or weekends. As a journalist, you will be called upon to report on the misadventures of the human race, so you will have to accustom yourself to speaking frequently to the victims and perpetrators of death, disaster, and destruction. At times, as you can well imagine, that can be unpleasant.

On the whole, however, I continue to be optimistic about the prospects for anthropologists in television journalism. I think anthropologists can, and should, find considerable satisfaction in communicating their insights and perspectives to a large and diverse audience, and television news offers one of the best means I know for accomplishing that goal. I regard television journalism as an important and appropriate field for applied anthropology. Television news will continue to play a major role in defining public issues and shaping public opinion; if anthropologists wish to be part of that process, they would do well to do so from the inside. Television journalists report every day on stories of vital anthropological interest—stories such as the spread of acquired immunodeficiency syndrome (AIDS), the crisis in child care, the degradation of the environment, the rise of fundamentalism, the changing role of women—stories that cry out for anthropological input. Ultimately, of course, what we really need are far more anthropological newsmakers, but I do not think another anthropological newscaster or two would hurt.

REFERENCES

Eiselein, E. B., and Martin Topper. 1976. "Anthropologists and Broadcasting: Roles and Entry Strategies." *Human Organization* 35: 157-164.

Hood, Stuart. 1987. *On Television*. 3d ed. London: Pluto.

Kottak, Conrad. 1990. *Prime-Time Society: An Anthropological Analysis of Television*. Belmont, CA: Wadsworth.

Lett, James. 1986. "Anthropology and Journalism." *Communicator* 40, no. 5: 33-35.

———. 1987a. "An Anthropological View of Television Journalism." *Human Organization* 46, no. 4: 356-359.

———. 1987b. "An Anthropologist on the Anchor Desk." *Practicing Anthropology* 9, no. 1: 2, 22.

Rosten, L. 1971. "A Disenchanted Look at the Audience." In *Radio and Television: Readings in the Mass Media*, edited by Allen and Linda Kirshner, 135-141. New York: Odyssey Press.

Chapter 9

The Anthropologist as Television Producer

Ira R. Abrams

INTRODUCTION

As both a professional anthropologist and a television producer, I have spent over 15 years working to bring anthropology to the public through the medium of television. While combining television and anthropology has always been an intriguing process, it has seldom been an easy one nor one that, as most know, has actually had much favor within anthropology as a whole. But regardless of how members of the discipline may feel about it, there is little question that television has, and will continue to provide anthropologists with, one of the most important means of communicating their message to the general public. This is a critical audience for anthropologists, for its opinion has a significant impact on the funding of anthropological research and, in many cases, the very survival of the people anthropologists study.

Over the years, I have met many other anthropologists who share my feelings about television and anthropology. As I served on panels at annual meetings of anthropologists or worked on television programs about other anthropologists and their work, I usually discovered that a good many were just as interested as I was in reaching the television-viewing public, but they lacked the background in television production to know how to make it happen. Consequently, they would often ask me how they might raise money for, or generate interest in, a special project they had long dreamed of doing for television. Like most of their colleagues, they dedicated themselves to communicating with their students, colleagues, and readers, but they simply did not understand the process and requirements of using television to reach a wider audience.

Ironically, most anthropologists who have worked regularly with film and video have restricted their efforts to producing a more scholarly and therefore acceptable "visual anthropology"— ethnographic and anthropological film and video—and have virtually ignored the possibilities of broadcast television.[1] For many, I am sure, broadcasting seemed an unnecessarily "popularist" approach to anthropology compared with the more "serious" uses of film and video in research and teaching. When anthropologist/filmmakers did think about television, they often naively assumed that there was little need to distinguish their own scholarly media approaches from those of broadcast television in general.[2] They were, after all, recording never-before filmed aspects of cultures that would no doubt disappear, and they often employed state-of-the-art film and video technology to do it. There was a sense that their pioneering film and video approaches to anthropology should be warmly received by those who produce television programming. But nothing could have been further from the truth, for there was a vast difference between the two approaches; what traditionally had worked for limited student and anthropological film festival viewing simply does not make good television. Rather, televised anthropology, or what I think we should be calling "broadcast anthropology," must be designed consciously for the medium of television and the nature of the vast number of potential viewers who may watch it.

The cost of the common conceits and misunderstandings that anthropologists usually have in placing anthropology on television has been particularly high for the field, for they have resulted in leaving the important concerns of broadcast anthropology to nonanthropologists—and the public's perception of anthropology has therefore generally been determined by outsiders. The complex understandings of the field and the general excitement of our discoveries are therefore often being reported third- and fourth-hand.

That this is the case is particularly surprising, for anthropologists have, since the very beginning of the discipline, authored their own ethnographies, ethnologies, site reports, and trade books and unflinchingly tried to interpret themselves and their ideas in print and at the podium to the general public. They have in fact been used as the principal intellectual glue that has held most broadcast anthropology programming together, and they have served with increasing regularity as on-camera scientific experts and off-screen content consultants. Yet, anthropologists are not generally the producers, the writers, the directors, or the on-air guides for broadcast anthropology.

Why shouldn't anthropologists be more of a driving force behind the design and/or making of programming that is so important to them? Why shouldn't they be capable of reaching television audiences in the same way they do the book-buying public?

Not too long ago television field production was quite expensive, and few stations would take a chance on a relatively untrained producer/writer. Today, however, the costs of acceptable broadcast quality field video are such that anthropologists clearly *can* produce material for broadcast if they wish. But to have their material aired and actually seen by television viewers, they must come to see television in a very different light than they generally have in the past. Television is not simply a vehicle for presenting cultural data or their own particular ideas about them, rather, it is a large business and creative endeavor whose professionals look at product almost exclusively in terms of broad audience appeal. Failure to understand that point has been a major problem for anthropologists who wished to use television to reach a wider audience.

The reality is that television is a world so different from the halls of academe that it should, for all practical purposes, be treated as another culture—one that needs to be examined with the same intensity and professional rigor that would be applied to any group whose ways at first defy easy comprehension.[3] If anthropologists fail to do this and to study how television works as a medium, television and its promise will continue to baffle them, and the presentation of anthropology on the air will remain the de facto domain of a limited number of professional television producers without appropriate anthropological sensitivity or background—and anthropologists will, by and large, continue to be left out of the process. Obviously, I do not think that this needs to be the case.

In looking back at my attempts to put anthropology on television, I think that some of my experiences may help to reveal a number of important approaches to this process. Such a recounting can, however, only scratch the surface, for my own story is only one of many, and even at that one's education in broadcast production is never really over, for television is a continually changing medium, and each new project brings with it important new lessons and approaches.

A FIRST ATTEMPT

Like all career beginnings, my own entry into television was marked by some notably instructive failures. It is a general truth in film and television that without doing a few bad productions you will never learn how to make a good one.

My first dealings with television occurred while I was a graduate student at Harvard University. I had worked as a photographer before going to graduate school and from the outset was intrigued by the prospects of using film to record and present what we knew of other cultures. Like many other anthropology students in the early 1970s, I was excited by the new vérité and "event/sequence" approaches to ethnographic filming. They, in fact, seemed so compelling to me that I could not understand why this new ethnographic film was not being widely shown on television. These were, after all, the real stories of human survival and cultural adaptation, and they dealt with dramatic situations that should fascinate anyone. Films such as *The Feast*, *Argument About a Marriage*, and *To Live with Herds* seemed to provide incredible glimpses into the remote worlds to which anthropology had such an exclusive access. Yet these films were shown only to small audiences of students in classrooms and other anthropologists who attended the occasional screenings at our yearly meetings. I could not understand why these films were receiving such a limited viewing.

My training in ethnographic film production at Harvard continued, revealing the difference between films made for the classroom and films made specifically for television. I took my first class in ethnographic film production from Robert Gardner, an extremely creative anthropological filmmaker who seemed inevitably to present the material about other cultures through the use of a *story*. I later studied informally with John Marshall and Timothy Asch, who produced the small films I had so admired—films that purposefully avoided a story and were, rather, about *small, discrete events and sequences of activity* within a culture.[4] Their approach was, in fact, completely in line with where anthropology was going at the time.[5] Unlike Gardner, they had at the time abandoned and denied as valid any attempt at representing a culture in its entirety in a single film. Only the presentation of a number of such small films could, they felt, allow an audience to have a more realistic picture of a society. Obviously there would need to be teachers and study guides to help them explain the missing pieces and provide the larger and necessary context. Like other ethnographic filmmakers of the time, they were particularly concerned with issues of subjectivity, reflexivity, and not imposing an etic, or non-indigenous, narrative structure on the films they made.[6]

As a student anthropologist I was excited by both approaches of Marshall-Asch and Gardner; yet, it never occurred to me that they would be so different in terms of their appropriateness for broadcast television. I learned this because my first attempt to make a film for television followed the Marshall-Asch model— the model that did not work for television.

THE JOSEPH AND LUCIA II

Before leaving Harvard, I decided, along with fellow graduate student Sanford Low, to produce an anthropological film about life on an Italian American fishing trawler out of Gloucester. With much care and attention to detail we completed a short observational film that documented one of its many yearly fishing trips. We shot it thanks to the gracious loan of a camera and outright gift of film stock by an incredibly generous John Marshall. After a week at sea and an appropriate editing period, we took our rough cut proudly to a small public broadcasting service (PBS) station in New Hampshire, where we fully expected to receive some expression of interest and appreciation for our effort. It was clearly a limited "observational" film, but it was also in the great tradition of Robert Flaherty—it was man against the seal!—and it dealt with one aspect of an important New England subculture. But our enthusiasm was not shared. We learned that we had produced a film that would not "work well" on television. We had thought that the simple act of observing an Italian American fishing crew living out their daily life at sea and dealing with the dramatic challenge of the elements would make compelling television viewing. Yet, when we were asked why a viewer should care or want to see it—what the *story* was—we could not come up with any acceptable answers for them or for ourselves.

We had learned one of our first lessons about putting anthropological material on television. Television requires a strong and immediate sense of "story"—a story with a beginning, a middle, and an end or, in terms of a traditional three-act dramatic structure, a setup, conflict, and resolution. It can be about an event, individual, or even the quest of an anthropologist to understand something. Ours was about a fishing trip and the way a group of men worked and lived together at sea—there had never been any thought given to a premise or the context that would make the program matter to a viewer. I have since come to realize that this premise must be established early in the program to tell the audience where they are going. Without a premise and a story, most material, even documentary material, rarely works for television.

For television it is extremely important that both these elements be easily summarized in no more than a single paragraph or so—the kind that you would find in *TV Guide*. It tells you right up front just why you should care. The premise in many anthropological programs might simply be that a strange, non-Western culture makes a great deal of sense when looked at from an anthropological perspective. It might also be about how the anthropologist overcame major difficulties, as usually happens, to come to that conclusion. Conflict and disagreement between anthropologists, which is never hard to find, make wonderful television if they can be explained in simple enough terms.

Generally, in the academic world, anthropologists describe their research in terms that their colleagues can understand. For potential television audiences they must do the same, by using a simple dramatic structure and a strong sense of premise.

THE LIVING MAYA

My next involvement with television production came almost a year after I had taken my first teaching job at Southern Methodist University (SMU). My dissertation research led me to work with Yucatec Maya in Mexico and Belize, and I had previously shot an ethnographic film on the Tzotzil Maya in the Chiapas highlands of Mexico. At SMU I had continued my interests in the Maya to such an extent that I decided to try to produce a one-hour program on the living Maya of today. My working premise was that in spite of the fact that most Americans thought the Maya had disappeared long ago, the present-day Maya were very much alive and shared a remarkable continuity with their ancient past. Clearly, understanding them would give us important clues as to what ancient Maya life was like.

To have a clear and forceful sense of vision about this program, I combined forces to collaborate with Grant Jones, a friend and fellow Maya specialist. We had decided to seek funding from the Media Program of the National Endowment for the Humanities and to aim the program at PBS for an existing series, if at all possible. This process led me to talk to Michael Ambrosino, then the executive producer of the "NOVA" series at WGBH-television in Boston. Ambrosino was far more helpful than most people in his position generally are because of his special interest in anthropology and a well-known penchant for helping young producers get started in the business.[7] He said that what we needed to get this show on the air was a good treatment that would help us get some funding, and he offered to provide the services of one of his writers for that purpose.

With a strong vérité documentary perspective, I had not, until that moment, given adequate thought to the necessity of having a good treatment prior to production. Potential funding from the National Endowment for the Humanities (NEH) Media Program, however, required a treatment and would provide successful applicants with money in two distinct stages: scripting and then production itself. We turned out a treatment with an accompanying proposal and applied for the first stage. After what seemed a very long time, we were turned down.

Our failure to receive a grant with such professional backing was dismaying. We discovered, however, that one of the reasons for the rejection of our proposal was that there had been a previous submission on virtually the same topic by well-known ethnographic filmmaker Hubert Smith (*The Spirit Possession of Alejandro Mamani, The Children Know*). Smith's proposal had won out for a number of good reasons. For one, he had a considerable documentary track record and an excellent reputation. Also, his proposal had worked hard to integrate what was then an important theoretical concern of anthropologists regarding the production of film—reflexivity (i.e., an attempt by the filmmaker to include his or her own subjective approach and goals with the film itself). He had also assembled a stellar advisory panel, which included Margaret Mead, theoretician Jay Ruby, and a number of other anthropological luminaries. Smith had also carefully sought political support for his project both in government and in academic circles. It was a solid and impressive application that had every right to be awarded. Yet Smith had never worked with the Maya, and we had!

The biggest irony was that within a short number of years, I would find myself as the principal anthropological adviser and an advisory panelist to the four-part television series Smith intended to produce from this Maya material. By the time Smith was done, he had shot over 160,000 feet (over 125 hours) of reflexive film and spent close to five years on his project.

I learned a number of important things from this experience. For one, writing for NEH grants is a long and frustrating endeavor. I would not try it again and certainly would not advise others to unless they had developed strong political and academic support for their project and had a lot of time on their hands. An alliance with a television station or producer is simply not enough to win a grant from a government agency. Also, you should never apply to just one agency if you are really serious about getting funding, no matter how wonderful you think your proposal is.

Such government-supported media projects are by their nature unwieldy devices that take a good deal more time and energy to build and hold together than they are probably worth. Moreover, such projects have many masters to please, and there are a good many places along the road where they can and do regularly fall apart. There are simply too many projects and too little money available. Proposals may fail to line up with the content interests of a particular funding round, or they may be shot down at the scripting proposal stage or at the production application stage. They can also die at the hands of unsympathetic academic reviewers, industry reviewers, or general audience reviewers. If you do make it through this marathon obstacle course, the chances of making any real money on such a project or having much control over it are remote; salaries are expected to be "reasonable," advisory panels must have a strong say as to content, and PBS distribution must be provided free of charge.

THE THREE WORLDS OF BALI

By 1976 my interests in television had grown to the point that I had been invited by Barbara Myerhoff, then chair of the Anthropology Department at the University of Southern California (USC), to go there to create a new program that would, among other things, teach students to produce material about anthropology for television. That program was eventually created under the aegis of USC's new Center for Visual Anthropology, which I founded. The center was set up to provide realistic training opportunities for our students, and just such an opportunity arose when I proposed to fellow anthropologist Steve Lansing that we teach an integrated summer field project in Indonesia that would provide training in both traditional social anthropology and ethnographic film production.

Shortly after Lansing and I began to plan this course, we found out that "Eka Dasa Rudra," a never-before-seen ritual that is performed only once each 100 years and which involves the entire island of Bali, was soon to take place, but it would be in the middle of the spring semester, long before our planned summer class. After considerable discussion we decided to seize this rare opportunity and try to recruit a mixed crew of professionals and a few available students to record the event. As we came to realize the potential importance of the documentary, it became clear that we should do everything we could to get our work on television, where it could be seen by as many people as possible. That had not been our original intention, for I knew how difficult it would be to get student work on the air, but it could, we reasoned, do much to further the center and its goals. Moreover, given the incredible circumstances of the event, I knew that there was a magnificent "hook"—the Balinese fully expected the world to end if they did not do this ceremony correctly. There was clearly a great deal of dramatic content here. All we had to do was to get professionals with their own equipment to go with us on a deferred basis, as well as find enough money to buy film and get to Bali.

Through my connections with Sam Low, now an associate producer on the "Odyssey" series, and Michael Ambrosino, now the executive producer of that series, I felt that I could at least check out one possible avenue of television exposure. I knew "Odyssey" both acquired and even occasionally coproduced programs, and I thought they might be interested in what we were about to shoot. Yet, I was quite concerned that they might not trust me, with so little experience in producing for television, to come back with what they wanted—a quality, hour-long program for prime-time broadcast. To try to provide answers to those questions, I flew to Boston.

Low and Ambrosino were intrigued but would make no commitment on an event that had not yet happened and a production team they knew nothing about. Nevertheless, they cautiously provided me with their principal guidelines, which included material with a strong sense of story and an easily identifiable premise. Two important considerations they had when acquiring material were (1) that the program should attempt to show and explain the work of an anthropologist in the field and (2) that it should, as much as possible, allow the subjects of the program to speak for themselves. Also—and this was quite important to them—the program should *look* like "an Odyssey." When I asked what they thought an "Odyssey" looked like, they said they were not quite sure, but they would know one when they saw it!

While I knew at that time that it would be virtually impossible to make a film about the entire Balinese culture, the folks at "Odyssey" seemed to be somewhat intrigued with that possibility. As my previous training in anthropology and ethnographic film production had shown me that films about specific events can help to reveal the process or organization of a society, I knew that this particular islandwide ceremony in Bali might do much the same for the entire Balinese culture. It would be without question an enormous challenge.

Armed with only a nod from "Odyssey" to look at the footage when we returned, we went to Bali with just enough funding from the center to purchase film and tape stock and our meals. Hard work and persistence had gotten us free airfare, free hotels, and most importantly, a professional film production crew—a cameraman and a soundman who would come on a deferred basis with their own equipment. A free trip to an exotic island to witness a ceremony no one alive had ever seen before—which promised the sacrifice of elephants, tigers, and supposedly every known animal in the world—proved enough of a draw to get the very cameraman who had worked with Hubert Smith on his Maya project and to get one of the best sound recordists in Los Angeles. By now, I hoped I knew a good story when I saw one! If not, I would have a hectic trip to Bali and a very short television career.

When we arrived in Bali, the once-solid preproduction treatment that I had labored over with Lansing had a distinctly hollow ring to it—many of the interesting characters Lansing had worked with during his many years in Bali turned out to be remarkably unphotogenic or otherwise inappropriate. Moreover, the vaunted ceremony appeared as if it was going to be a much lesser event than we had imagined. An elephant was to be sacrificed—but in Sumatra, and its blood shipped to the ceremony by air. The tiger turned out to be a small ocelot. Worse, kittens, puppies, and a full-grown eagle were to be sacrificed. No American audience could watch that kind of carnage.

But soon other aspects of the event suddenly took on far more importance than we had imagined. We knew that when the Balinese had been forced to do the "Eka Dasa Rudra" 17 years early by the president of Indonesia for tourism reasons, the volcano where the temple sat had blown up on the very first day of the event—what we did not know was that the high priest who was responsible for scheduling that ill-timed event had refused to talk to anyone about the fiasco since then. Sadly, the dalang, a shadow puppeteer on whom we had hoped to focus, had died in a tragic motorcycle accident just before we arrived. But we discovered his widow was now suddenly devoting herself to learning his craft. More importantly, she had recently been informed by a priest that her husband had died because the gods had called him to perform before them for the very event we were about to film. Clearly these events and possibilities were not a part of our original scenario, but, on a gut level, they seemed to me to be extremely compelling as possible subject matter for the film, for they helped to build a larger story that gave the event an incredibly powerful sense of *personal meaning*. I felt we should interview both individuals as soon as we could. Even though Lansing was especially shocked that I wanted to interview the newly widowed puppeteer's wife, I knew that I could not leave if I did not follow through on these opportunities to connect the viewing audience to the Balinese on such an emotional level. I knew that I had to return with a story not only that made sense but that people could also care about. Remarkably, both the widow and the priest very much wanted to tell their stories.

Later, while we were preparing to shoot the main events of the ceremony, I happened briefly to catch the end of a broadcast on Balinese television of a high priest explaining to the Balinese themselves what would happen at the ceremony and what it would mean for them. Again, I felt this might not only be compelling material but also fulfill Low's request that we have the Balinese speak for themselves—and in this case, in a particularly competent and sophisticated way. Abandoning every vérité convention I knew of, I arranged to have the priest and the entire television crew *repeat* their broadcast in the studio the following week, using the same script that they had on the original broadcast.

When the ceremony was over and we were finally to leave Bali, I shot as much cutaway material as I could on the way to the airport of daily Balinese life. I was just beginning to feel that the event and the individuals we had recorded were providing us with the framework for a broader anthropological documentary on Balinese culture and society itself—something I had at first doubted we could, or even should try to, make.

When we returned to the States, I hired an editor for a short time to put together a small amount of our material to show to the "Odyssey" people. They were fascinated with what we had come back with. We had purposely filmed Steve Lansing as anthropologist moderating many of the events that were unfolding. We had a lot of Balinese telling their own stories—in *five* different languages. Michael Ambrosino was impressed, though still hesitant, but two small development grants and a good deal of preliminary editing later, we had a commitment from "Odyssey" for a show.

Editing took a lot of time. The many languages to translate in the program gave us a lot of trouble, and at times making a coherent and credible single show about an entire culture as complex as the Balinese seemed absurd. When we were having trouble editing, Ambrosino would remind me that editing problems were usually story problems. He was right. It took four separate people working hard on the script to make it work. We had an editor whose sense of story and energy was quite strong. Yet, in spite of her patience and creativity, I was, in the end, forced to replace her because the executive producer felt that she had been cutting with "too strong a hand" and her work would not match the more metered, standard television tone that he had established for the other shows in the series. It was a painful decision for me to dismiss a valued and critical team member—and by now, good friend—or lose the show. It is not hard to see where you stand in the hierarchy when you are forced to make a decision like that. Yet, it was a decision that came from the executive producer's many years of television experience, and it had to be respected.

In the end, as well as the technical experience I gained, I

learned that nothing in television ever gets done without an incredible amount of stress and risk taking. One risks creative and financial failure over and over again at a number of key stages. In our case, we had gone to Bali with no assurance that we would come back with enough good material to make a compelling "promo" reel for "Odyssey" and therefore have the resources to finish our film. Moreover, had the program not been picked up by "Odyssey" and had we been able to finish it on our own, our chances for airing it in the United States would have been quite remote. Television programmers usually seek a number of programs that can be fitted, as a series, into regular, ongoing time slots. There is no place for a single documentary that is not a celebrity-packed special. They simply do not sell. Either there must be enough shows (three or more) to make up a series, or they must find a home in an existing series such as "Odyssey."[8]

From producing this program, I learned, more than anything else, that a television production is the work of a lot of people who all must do their best if the show is to succeed. The terms *producer* or *director* never come close to accounting fully for the intellectual and creative accomplishments of a show—television production is truly a collaborative art involving a lot of people. That is what in the end hooked me on television production. There was a "high" that came from the group process as well as from the opportunity to be personally creative within it. All of this was set against the risk of failure—failure to come back with the goods, to make something of it once you did, and in doing that to meet a very real air date.

The resulting program, *The Three Worlds of Bali*, became a popular part of the "Odyssey" series and went on to win a CINE Golden Eagle Award. Because free off-air taping was allowed, it has been used extensively by anthropology classes throughout the country and has served as an important educational tool for introductory courses. It was recently voted by the students of USC's Center of Visual Anthropology one of the best anthropological films ever made. Yet, the completion of *The Three Worlds of Bali* did not come without many other nonmonetary costs—the greatest cost being my job at USC.

Because the scope and approach of our show broke a lot of

new ground for the series, "Odyssey" was never quite sure exactly what format the show should have. What would it take for them to "know" this was an "Odyssey"? Did they need maps? Should there be animation to show how the complicated temple system worked? Should they really show an eagle—the American totemic symbol—having its throat slit, even if it was going on to a better life with its new karma?

Questions like these required my recutting or revising the show a total of three times, once with the new editor who had been picked for me. It was a process that I later learned is not all that unusual in documentary production. But the chairman of my department was no longer Barbara Myerhoff, who knew a good deal about film, and he decided that no movie should take as long to complete as this one was taking and that I should stop it right then and there and get back to the serious work of teaching. I was caught in the middle of two opposing forces, for there was a contract between the series and the university for me to finish the film. Of course, I could not abandon a film in which I had invested so much energy and that I had made so many commitments to others to finish. I also believed in the film and felt that the Balinese and our center had much to gain from its successful completion. Faced with either finishing the film or being fired, I chose the former.

FACES OF CULTURE

The decision to leave academic anthropology was a difficult one, yet it made me available for another unexpected opportunity to deal with anthropology and television. With a successfully completed television program and the extensive knowledge I had of anthropological footage from teaching ethnographic film over the years, I applied for the position of series producer of a troubled 26-part anthropology telecourse at a public television station. I had found the listing in a classified ad in the *Los Angeles Times*. The Bali show and my background in anthropology got me the job.

If I thought that the "Odyssey" film had fully prepared me to make a series for television, I soon found out otherwise. Once when I was in Boston, Michael Ambrosino told me that he had never taken on a project that had not been a little bit beyond his reach. The executive producer at the television station knew enough to know that I was going to need some real help on this one. Only two weeks of preparation time were left before production needed to begin, for the series had lain dormant for at least eight months after the original producer and writer had been fired. The station hired a seasoned pro, Arthur Barron, to serve as my creative consultant and build a staff that would meet the unique requirements of the production deadlines we faced. In a surprising way, the series represented everything I had wanted to do while working at USC. As American moviemaker Steven Spielberg once said, the project allowed me to put sprocket holes on my imagination. The series was to be made primarily from acquired footage, yet the more than 200 hours of anthropological films they had amassed to look at contained mostly high school and home movie titles like *A Boy's Life in Ghana* and *Pygmie Madness*. Most of the people with sources of good footage had been leery of including their material in a series where the subjects they filmed could be exploited or put in a bad light by being taken out of context. My arrival on the scene changed a lot of that. There was often a general relief at dealing with a "simpatico" anthropologist.

Perhaps the biggest problem we faced was that, as the series was intended to be a telecourse in the United States as well as general progamming in Canada and overseas, it had to have both a strong textbook tie-in as well as a good deal of entertainment value. One of the ways I solved this dilemma was to create two different types of shows; 18 of them would follow the text as much as possible, covering one or more chapters in a single half-hour segment—what I called our "omnibus" shows—and eight shows would be case studies devoted to either a single culture or a single issue. A strong story line could be built into these programs, which could be made interesting beyond the scope of the text. What I had in mind was to reprise or remake a number of anthropological classics I liked and felt were a turn-on to anthropology. We arranged for Napoleon Chagnon to serve as the writer and work with an editor to make a new, shorter version of *A Man Called Bee*. He was a natural and adapted quite naturally to the process.

The Anthropologist as Television Producer

The other shows that we did as case studies were remakes of *Trobriand Cricket*, *The Spirit Possession of Alejandro Mamani*, *Always for Pleasure*, which was combined with another film on the Black Indians of New Orleans, and a film called *WOW*, which had been made on the Asmat of New Guinea. *Santiago de Chuchumatan* and *Appeals to Santiago* were combined to make another case study on economic anthropology, and *The Children Know* and other Hubert Smith–produced Aymara material were combined to make a show on stratification. We also contracted with Hubert Smith to recut and condense the four-hour-long Yucatec Maya shows (*The Living Maya*), on which I had previously worked with him, into a single 28-minute case study on marriage and the family. Smith himself felt that, in the end, the tightening process had provided him with a much stronger, single-focus show of which everyone was proud.

Barron and I set up a staff of five writer-editor teams to develop and finish each show. They worked on computer-assisted off-line editing systems that we purchased especially for the series. They speeded up the editing process a great deal and make our on-line time minimum. The idea was that I was to function as something like a "chief anthropologist" who would sit down with the writers and tell them how I wanted each show to which they were assigned to be written. I told them what I thought the story was and, if present, what the overriding premise was. I usually did this after first talking with the series instructional designer. She was responsible for making sure that the text and series lined up with reasonable precision and, if necessary, telling us it was OK to depart from the text, as it could be covered in other materials. She was a particularly important part of the entire process, and I came to value her insights and in-depth understanding of the educational process.

After pitching my version of the content of each show with the writers, I gave them what film material I thought was available and should be used to tell that story. I gave them far more visual material than they actually needed so as to allow them to make as much of their own statement as possible. They were also free to request additional material and to contact the textbook's author and any specialists to whom they might want to talk. They were then given a short deadline to come up with program treatments. Once their treatments were approved, the writer, editor, and I sat down together and reviewed the revised treatment and the material the writer thought would work. I exercised veto power and often suggested other material, as did the editor, who had often seen material from other shows that was more appropriate.

Each writer had some documentary screenwriting credits, but we looked for ability to handle dramatic content as well. A number of our writers came directly from screenwriting programs at major universities. We purposefully chose editors who were known to be strong on story and who had worked primarily in film. Most of the material we were working with came from films but was transferred to video and edited in video. Most of the editors needed to be trained in electronic editing but responded quickly to the difference between clipping film apart and making electronic cuts. Their ability to receive this valuable training while working with us helped us obtain some very good film editors at a very reasonable rate.

Throughout production, a number of difficult issues that could affect our credibility as an anthropology series needed to be worked out between the station and us. One was the issue of script approval by the anthropologists who supplied so much of our material. Another was the issue of whether the station should impose traditional American standards about nudity on the material shown in the series. Perhaps the most critical issue, however, was whether subtitles should be used rather than voice-over translation when the subjects in the films spoke to us. On each of these issues, the station's position was the opposite of ours, and I had to take a stand that often put me at some risk in order to change existing policy.

In most cases, suppliers of material were friends or colleagues and were willing to accept my script decisions, as a credible anthropologist, as the final ones. The station could not afford the time or money to finish a show whose script (and possibly the images themselves) would have to be changed at the last minute. The nudity issue was finally resolved when our instructional designer took a strong stand that definitions of nudity were themselves examples of cultural relativism and that the series could not reasonably represent its anthropological content if nudity were removed. The fact that we would not be broadcast

The Anthropologist as Television Producer

on commercial prime time also helped on this one. The subtitle issue was resolved by sheer persistence—it seemed to me the only way really to experience the people who were on the screen and to allow them to speak for themselves. We decided, however, to use good subtitles—large, clear, and with "drop-shadow" (outlined) whenever possible. Hubert Smith's *Living Maya* series provided an excellent example for us of what could be done with subtitles.

One other issue did not necessarily affect our credibility but did at first give me some concern—whether to use a celebrity narrator or not. The station felt quite strongly that we should, and I think that in the end they were right. Even PBS is concerned with ratings and the marketability of their product, and like all commercial stations, they feel that a celebrity narrator or host can be a big draw. For an anthropology series, such a person can serve as a familiar culture broker who can motivate an audience to watch often difficult material.

We searched long and hard for an appropriate celebrity narrator and ended up with David Carradine of "Kung Fu" fame. I was much more interested in Christopher Plummer, who had expressed a willingness to work with us, but I could record him only in New York City. As our $1.5 million project was moving at an incredible pace, two productions per month to meet our scheduled air date, my executive producer simply would not allow me to leave the Los Angeles area. Working with Carradine provided a whole new set of revelations, most of them having to do with the inherent difficulty of working with a celebrity who is by definition always busy. Tardiness was to be expected. Limos were required. Script interpretation often demanded lengthy discussion when the actor felt strongly that his way of presenting an issue was better than what was on the page. Often he was right, but often I was too. I learned that a narrator's interpretation of the script may often make just as important a contribution to the whole as an editor or cameraperson does. Though narrators work for relatively short periods of time, they are definitely a part of the production team. Carradine and I became good friends for that time, and in the end, I was very pleased with what a trained voice and committed personality could bring to the narration of such a series. I consider working with Carradine an important part of my education in television.

We spent a remarkably small amount of money on the production of *Faces of Culture*. It worked out to be only about $27,000 per show. Comparable productions were running $75-$150,000 per episode.[9] Our ability to work so efficiently and cheaply was helped a lot by an efficient research and acquisitions staff as well as a strong associate producer and production manager. The pilot show cost us considerably more than any of the other programs, for with it we worked out our format, operating procedures, and the series opening. I learned, in particular, that you should not skimp on the series opening. It not only pulls in your audience and makes them want to watch your show, but its musical score, energy, and content express over and over again the quality and scope of your series. We spent $5,000 for the original music of our opening alone, and it was worth every penny.

By the time I came on board, almost half of the $1.5 million budgeted for the series and its educational support had been spent on a failed pilot show, for which the original producer and writer had been fired. The original pilot had turned out to be virtually a slide-tape show with heavy-handed, redundant narration that told viewers exactly what they were seeing. Our approach was to use self-contained sequences and events, à la Marshall and Asch, to make our points and use sparse narration to tie these sequences together into as much of a story as we could. It is not easy for a series to find its voice. It is even harder for one to be anthropologically credible and create strong viewer interest. In spite of what I felt was often a product of mixed quality, the series won favorable review in the *American Anthropologist* and was awarded both an Emmy and an Ohio State Award. While there are many shows that I would like to do over again if I had the chance, that is never possible with the fast pace of television. We actually produced our first show, *The Nature of Anthropology*, in little more than a week from start to finish! Films are, as they say, never finished; they are only "released." Working in television provides daily examples of that.

RIPLEY'S BELIEVE IT OR NOT

After the *Faces* series was completed, I worked on two other PBS series, which dealt with science as well as anthropology, and Columbia Television's *Ripley's Believe It or Not*, a series for commercial television.

On *Ripley's*, I was a film researcher. At first I thought that this was going to be a frivolous series and that surely I would now have my membership card as an anthropologist pulled. Yet I soon discovered that virtually all of the other *Ripley's* research staff also had Ph.D.'s and many were active scholars in their own right. Moreover, all the series producers seemed to be deeply concerned with the accuracy and impact of their material. One had, in fact, been a past series producer for *The National Geographic Specials*.

The series needed a steady supply of what was referred to in-house as "ooga booga"—film and tape examples of unusual cultural practices and rituals. Whenever enough of these examples fitted into a coherent theme such as "water rites," a four–five-minute rites and rituals act was added to that week's show.

I reviewed material sent by acquisitions scouts throughout the world, negotiated to obtain footage for potential act material, and then attempted to put a story spin on what I had in order to "sell" it to whoever of the five series-segment producers needed an act that week.[10] To my surprise, I found that the series producers were quite concerned with their own credibility and that of the series. They always expected us to verify facts carefully and triple-check sources.

I learned several important lessons about television and anthropology at *Ripley's*. I learned how crucial a narrative hook can be in presenting anthropology to the public. As it was essentially a magazine format show, *Ripley's* sequences were usually no more than three or four minutes in length, seldom more than five or six. I came to realize that if there was a good story there, it really could be effectively told in that amount of limited time. If you could not crystallize your story hook in a sentence or two as I had to when pitching segment ideas, you probably did not have a good story that would hold the attention of their enormous audience. It had taken me over a year and a half to come up with that sentence or two for the *Bali* film. I decided that in the future I would not begin such an enterprise without having that sentence or two clear in my own mind from the very beginning.

I also learned that in order to generate the quick interest that you must have in a medium where there are many other instant program options, the material for a television program must be highly visual and have lots of close-ups. The material should, in fact, work pretty well with the sound turned off. Most older ethnographic films were shot for the wide screen and did not, unfortunately, pay much attention to close-ups. A "tight head shot," in fact, appears virtually life-size on a normal television screen. Clearly, "whole bodies, whole acts" does not work well for television; people are remarkably small in a wide shot that is used in television and are very difficult to see. Additionally, I got the feeling that using a tripod or other camera support, rather than hand-holding a camera, gave static footage that had low energy for television. After hundreds of hours of looking at footage from around the world, I still find myself being drawn into hand-held material more of the time. Perhaps it is because camera people are forced to shoot a lot closer without support, and they and the people they film are free to move about—and that movement helps to build energy.

After the *Ripley's* series, I returned to produce segments for a PBS series in India, Italy, England, Guatemala, and the United States, and wrote and did some production management for an IMAX feature on the cultures of Indonesia.

TODAY AND TOMORROW

At this point in my career one thing about television has become quite clear to me: it is, above all else, a business, and to succeed in it and effectively present anthropological material to large television audiences, I must produce my own projects either by myself or in partnership with others. There are a number of experienced producers of broadcast anthropology who do that quite regularly; most of them, however, are doing so in countries other than the United States, countries where documentary programming is more widely accepted and anthropology is held in a higher regard.[11]

I am presently working on the development of two series about anthropology and anthropologists. In each, I have chosen an anthropologist who has something extremely important to say about which I can really care. In one case I have optioned a book, on which I hope to base a series, and in another, I have formed a joint venture between the author and myself to exploit her book as a series.[12] I know that it will be a gamble to get even one of these projects produced. But as I mentioned earlier, television is, above all else, an endeavor involving a great deal of risk. Yet by trying to create my own series, I hope not only to place ideas and perspectives I value before the public but also to share in the often significant revenues that can come from ownership of a successful television product.[13] And such revenue should, of course, allow me to produce more anthropologically oriented material for television.

Unfortunately, the process of *independent* television production requires a number of other skills and a good deal of extra knowledge that I have not had time to discuss here. These complexities must be saved for another chapter in another book.

There is no question that today it is becoming a great deal easier to put anthropology on television, especially in the new burgeoning cable markets. In the past five years, the expansion of cable television has provided hundreds of hours of air time for desperate station programmers to fill. The Discovery Channel, for instance, which is dedicated to nonfiction programming, acquires and packages many disparate one-hour and 30-minute-long single shows into aggregate series with general tags such as "Survival," "Adventure," and so on. Anthropologists who want to produce for television must study and become familiar with these trends and opportunities.

There still remains one large and unanswered question for me to address: if producing broadcast anthropology takes one on as difficult a journey as I have described, why then would anyone in their right mind want to travel that road? I can answer that question only for myself. For me it is the chance that I may generate an excitement and interest in anthropology for a great number of people and that in doing so, I may thereby help to make ours a better world to live in, a world in which the human spirit and its remarkable variation within culture are celebrated rather than attacked for their differences.

I am talking here about creating for others who have not been exposed to anthropology in a formal way the same compelling perspective of cultural relativism that got each of us involved with anthropology in the first place. What is it that made us want to know more? What is it that we can say as anthropologists about the human condition that can help us live together on this planet with our many unique and equally valuable ways of dealing with the world and its ever-present problems? This is what broadcast anthropology can and must address.

Today, in the 1990s, we may be on the verge of a belated human renaissance of sorts—a celebration of, and a growing global concern for, the people and things of this earth. There is now an ecological awareness that includes not only the land and the sea but the survival of the different peoples and cultures whose relationship with the planet now seems more important to us in the Western world than we would have ever thought before.

The greatest thing about television today is that we huddle around it not just for entertainment and escape but for a feeling of global community that can be instantly felt and can give our existence an all-important sense of meaning. The importance of anthropology and the sustenance it can bring to that community can, and should, be illuminated brightly and substantively by anthropologists themselves for those enormous, inquiring audiences gathered at the screen—whether they know it or not—to be moved and touched and inspired to understand.

NOTES

1. This has not been the case completely in Great Britain, where there has been a great deal more interest in putting on the air what is often closer to true ethnographic film. Notable anthropologist-producers such as Melissa Llewelyn-Davies, whose "Masai Diary" was an enormous success, and Andre Singer, past producer of the "Disappearing World" series, have managed to put some very serious anthropology on the air. The Granada Center for Visual Anthropology, directed by Paul Henely and David Turton, continues to interface in a credible manner between broadcast television in Great Britain and the world of serious anthropology.

2. See especially Sabin Jell-Bahlsen, "Funding Anthropological Film and Video Productions," *CVA Newsletter* (October 1988): 24-31.

3. Ibid.

4. John Marshall's early and later films did, however, deal quite effectively with story. *The Hunters*, which appropriately was produced

with Robert Gardner, had a strong, if not true, story line, and *!Nai: The Story of a !Kung Woman* may well be one of the finest anthropological stories yet told.

5. This was precisely what Max Gluckman and the other members of his "Manchester school" were trying to do with their "extended case method" and "situational analysis" approaches. They felt that they would be able to understand the larger process of social organization in a community only by recording the discrete interactions and events within a community over time. This would show which alternative institutions or values were used in different situations and would help the ethnographer to map out a truer diachronic picture of actual social process.

6. John Marshall did manage partially to overcome the constraints of this dictum with his masterful film *!Nai: The Story of a !Kung Woman*, which he made for the "Odyssey" series, about 25 years in the life of a !Kung woman he had filmed since childhood.

7. Television is, much more than film, a "producer's medium," for, in television production, a "director" is no more than a floor technician and/or control room director. The producer provides the bulk of the intellectual and creative drive for a television program, often serving as its writer as well.

8. Today, this is still the case for commercial and public television, though cable television has utilized a number of looser series formats to allow it to acquire a broader range of single shows. They pay remarkably little, however—and never enough to cover the actual expenses of production. Foreign television is not as difficult a market for single documentary programs today, and a good deal of the costs of production can be realized from a good production that has a reasonable amount of political content, which European audiences require.

9. *The Three Worlds of Bali*, although an hour-long program, cost considerably less and was a bargain for the series. While the shows they were producing themselves (nonacquisitions) cost between $225,000 and $325,000 each (an average figure for a PBS hour-long, original footage documentary at that time), our program cost them somewhere between $40,000 and $60,000 to complete, and unlike a straight acquisition of a finished program ($120,000-$40,000), they were able to have a great deal to say about how it was made.

10. I was astonished to find how much more film of bizarre behavior came from Japan than all other sources combined. In one segment I found that the people of two entire villages battered each other over the head with long bamboo poles for their annual celebration of their traditional hatred of one another. In another, businessmen hung like bats, wings and all, from trees until they dropped from exhaustion. There is clearly a lively side of Japanese culture that has not yet been fully

explored on television. From New Guinea came footage of adolescents rubbing their foreheads raw in a sensuous courtship ritual. My greatest treasure, however, was the information that Joan of Arc had not been burned at the stake but had actually gone to Switzerland and married instead. It is the truth! In the end, I think that I may have actually learned more about anthropology from working on this series than I did in formal classes at Harvard.

11. Others who have done this include Andre Singer, whose London partnership InCA has produced many independent documentaries and series; Hubert Smith, producer of *The Living Maya*; Sam Low, *The Navigators*; Dave Kendall, *Sunshine Journey*. The Granada television series *Disappearing World* has, and still does, actively seek proposals from anthropologists for programs based on their own work.

12. The first step toward producing your own programs or series is one of the most critical in the process of independent television production: acquiring the television rights to whatever it is you wish to produce. These rights become your "property." Most producers will not purchase these rights until they are sure that there is a market for the project and hence funding to produce it. They will therefore pay for an exclusive option to purchase the material at a later date, usually for 10 percent of its purchase price. Such options give producers the right to represent the property as being theirs and to use it to develop programming. Most producers will seek an initial free six-month option to allow them to "test the waters."

13. Working for PBS is particularly unfair to producers since most PBS producers also serve as writers, and PBS (known alternately as Poverty Broadcasting System) is not signatory to the Writers Guild and does not therefore pay residuals for reruns as commercial stations do. Additionally, unshared revenues are often made from sales outside the normal PBS window of exposure from syndication, cassette, and foreign sales. Likewise, producers do not receive a share of the often significant monies made from telecourse and textbook sales as well as from a specially published "readers guide" for the series.

Chapter 10

The Anthropologist as Radio Producer

Ken C. Erickson

Anthropologists looking for low-cost dissemination of their scientific or humanistic findings would do well to listen to the radio. While the English language directs us to use visual metaphors to mark perception or understanding, it is only since the advent of writing that the oral/aural channel has taken second place as a means of human discovery and sharing (Goody 1987). Television seems to have made things worse for the human voice, but the popular utility of the aural channel remains undiminished in radio broadcasting.

While a recent search of the catalogs at the Museum of Broadcasting in New York City did not turn up any documentary evidence of an early connection between anthropology and radio, there are a number of anecdotal accounts, usually of anthropologists being interviewed about their books. Walter Goldschmidt has reported on his radio work in the 1950s (Goldschmidt 1988). Listening to Denver's KOA radio one recent spring evening in western Kansas, I heard a local anthropologist commenting on the cross-cultural implications of Earth Day. Clearly, anthropology and radio are not strangers to one another.

Radio is more than the sum of its sounds. It is a product and a process. As a kind of social organization, a kind of institution, radio takes many different structural forms around the world and in the United States. By understanding how radio in the United States works, U.S. anthropologists may be able to make better use of it for dissemination of anthropological information. This chapter draws on my own 13 years of on-again, off-again experience in radio in small, medium, and large "markets" in Boston, Washington State, Kansas, and Wyoming; it is an effort to provide a foundation for a media anthropology of radio, grounded in a desire not only to use the medium for anthropological dissemination but to generate a better understanding of how radio works. Doing so may provide anthropologists with some of the information that they need to use radio more effectively.[1]

GETTING THE STORY ACROSS: LOCAL MARKETS

Getting the story across depends on the kind of story that you want to tell and on the kind of radio station available for your use. If you hoped to hear your anthropological insights on the radio, but your ideas ended up in the producer's "round file," it is possible that "you just don't know how radio works!" (Firesign Theater 1971).

Staff Mobility and Specialization

Radio's institutional culture is characterized by the high geographic (if not always social and economic) mobility of the people who practice it and by greater specialization in individual roles and intended audience from small to large markets. The local news and public affairs director in charge of an entire station's news and information this month may be on her way to produce a four-hour talk show in a "big market" station next month. Long-term relationships do form among broadcasters, but interpersonal networks tend to span a great deal of territory because people in the profession move so often.[2] This means that it may be possible to follow up on an anthropological idea a year or more after a project is finished, but you may do so with a new producer, a new program director, or a new news director. It also means that if you keep track of relationships in the industry, you may find wider audiences for your future work as your radio contacts spread out to other, bigger markets in the radio world. With more anthropologists developing long-term collaborative relationships with communities (Chambers 1987), radio broadcasters' high mobility may be put to good use.

Radio is also characterized by "window" or "niche" marketing—the practice of targeting a station's audio product toward a narrow market segment. Music stations adjust their product by adjusting their "mix"—their mixture of kinds of music, news, and talk—to attract more listeners in their targeted market segment. Quarterly audience measurements, conducted by market research firms, provide regular feedback to station managers. Large markets contain many stations, with most of them targeting a slightly different market segment. Smaller markets contain stations with more diversity in their product. Small-town stations do local news and interview programs and may even program a variety of music styles. Large stations are more often wedded to particular "formats."

Format is a kind of folk classification that is reproduced by industry publications like *Radio and Records* or *Billboard*, by market researchers, and by broadcasters talking shop over their typewriters (more often talking over their computer terminals, these days). The distinction among "CHR" (Current Hit Radio), "Top 40" (a station playing the top 40 current hits in frequent rotation), "AOR" (Album-Oriented Rock), and "Gold" (oldies but goodies) may not be salient to anthropologists wanting to disseminate scientific findings. For applied anthropologists seeking a particular audience, however, the distinctions can be very important. Because formats change and even disappear over time, checking with a local broadcaster can help you reach the right audience.

Putting that advice into practice suggests that format may not be the critical issue. The critical issue is contact with people in the radio industry. Here, the distinctions of scale among small, medium, and large market radio stations make a difference. The three categories present different opportunities for anthropologists wanting to use radio.

Small Markets

Small markets are those not included in the U.S. Department of Commerce list of standard metropolitan statistical areas

(SMSAs). In a small market radio station, the news director may also be the morning music show host. On weekdays, the morning show is called "morning drive" or "drive time," when radio's automobile commuter audience gives them their largest daily audience. Then, the station commands its highest advertising rates. In small markets, this may be the best arena for dissemination of anthropological findings.

Some small market stations maintain strong traditions of community service. These stations may have a farm show in the early morning; local news during morning drive and music; and a women's program, a gardening show, or a community bulletin board in the late morning. Applied anthropologists working with small communities may find themselves on live morning radio, sipping coffee and sharing a single microphone with the program host, and making comments on immigrant farm labor between country music and feed store commercials. A few minutes in front of a local microphone, explaining the nature of planned research or an applied project can be a useful step in building rapport with a field site. Access to the local program demands listening to the station, understanding the audience it is trying to reach (farmers? small communities? young people? Latinos?), and presenting your desire to be on the air to the appropriate person.

In a small market, the local program producer is probably also the program host and may also be the news director, farm director, news editor/reader, and morning personality. Call and ask the receptionist to let you speak to any of these. Small stations, if they put out any local news at all, are nearly always hungry for a story.

Medium Markets

Medium markets usually have greater job specialization within their radio stations. There are also greater format diversity in a medium market and a better chance that one or more stations emphasize news and information. Usually these are AM stations, but do not overlook the fact that many music-oriented formats on the FM band include short segments of talk or news; many feature longer public affairs programs on weekends.

Medium market stations usually have a news director who is responsible for news and public affairs programming. Medium market stations are often worried about their "book"—how well their numbers look in their quarterly audience surveys—so they may be less likely than small market stations to take programming risks. If your topic is interesting, timely, or a bit exotic, you may at least expect an expression of interest from most medium market stations.

Find the stations that seem most likely to present news or issues important to your anthropological project. Ask about the target audiences of stations that you wish to use for public service announcements for your applied project. Use your knowledge of the local area, the "market," and your best radio etiquette (discussed later) to get access to local "air time."

Bigger Markets

The top 50 radio markets in the United States encompass a stunning diversity of formats and target audiences. The specialization of stations in big markets presents special opportunities for anthropologists.

For example, if dissemination of a colleague's research on women's health in a Latino neighborhood is the focus, and you want to share what has been learned with that community, do not expect a 30-second story with a recorded sound bite from your health clinic to get your message across. If the story is important to the station's non-Latino audience, they may get the short message. If you can get in touch with a talk show producer, you might manage a 20-minute or longer segment on a talk show (and if your research is interesting to the health clinic, it is probably interesting to the talk show producer). But you will not reach much of your Latino audience. What are the options?

First, find the stations that use locally produced programming. Call and visit with the people in news or public affairs and ask them to do a story on your project. Try to appear on the air during a show placed at a time that your audience will listen. Targeting Latino workers in the electronics industry on a morning country and western show will not be effective if workers take the bus and work during the second shift at the plant. Your audience may not listen at work, but they may listen to Spanish-language programming. Learning the radio listening habits of your intended audience provides an opening for an interesting conversation with radio station producers. Your knowledge can be a "gift" with which you can win a broadcaster's rapport, just as in any field situation (Johnson 1984).

Next, you may decide that the research has general health policy implications. Find out where the major talk and information stations are. Listen to find a station with a program that might contain information about health policy. Try to write down exactly what you will share and why it is of general interest to the station's audience. If your insights are new or controversial, write that down, too. It may help sell your idea to the station. Then call the producer of the shows that you have identified. You can always catch the producer of a particular show during that show's air time. Ask the producer if your idea would fit with their program and follow up with a note.

If your research has produced significant, newsworthy findings, you may want to explore the possibility of doing (or having someone else do) a radio news story on your project. The key is newsworthiness. There is no hard-and-fast rule that distinguishes "news" from "feature" or "process" stories. (A process story is one that focuses on the process of how some work was done, rather than on the findings or outcomes.) Some stations are interested in both process and "hard" news, but most will be interested in the news value of your story. Is what you want to share really new? Does it have wider implications? Is it interesting? Are *you* interesting, and are *you* able to speak about your work in an interesting way? A yes answer to any three of these will probably get the interest of a news director.

If the story is interesting enough, the local news director may "feed" the story to a regional or national network. Again, there is considerable variety in local connections to wider networks of audio dissemination. There are news and public affairs networks for Spanish-language stations, for African American stations, and for sports or business or agricultural stations, among others. The local anthropologist can find out how the local station is connected to these wider networks.

There is still another possibility: the talk radio call-in show.

The key to getting on the air in talk radio, according to one major market executive producer, is to be "creative, upbeat, intelligent, witty, and short-winded."[3] The host depends on the producer to provide "talent"—in this case, a talented anthropologist who will hold audience attention. Producers do not like to be glared at through the studio window by disappointed program hosts.

NATIONAL DISSEMINATION

Even in the smallest markets, nearly every station has a national network affiliation. Networks offer a variety of services able to match specific formats and audience targets. ABC, for example, offers several hourly news services, each with its own program length and style designed to fit different local needs. Some network offerings use feature-length stories, some offer extended talk show formats, and some provide only "actuality cuts," short tape recordings of news makers with or without a "wrapper," an introduction by a radio news reporter.

Short News Stories

Radio newspersons in small markets enjoy hearing their own byline on the national network "feed." If the station in the market where you do your research has a national network affiliation, and your archaeological dig has discovered new evidence of human responses to climatic change in the region, you may be able to get national coverage of your findings through the local news producer. This will amount to a one-minute "actuality" (a sound bite) on national radio. In most cases, that is all that can be expected from commercial networks.

For an anthropological story to get more than a few minutes of national distribution, it must, at present, get the attention of noncommercial radio producers. National Public Radio (NPR) specializes in the longer stories that anthropological work most often generates. A regular press release from a university or a research organization may not get the attention of the national desk at NPR in Washington, but a letter from a researcher might do so. If the story piques the editor's interest, NPR may produce a story on the topic to include in one of its daily feature or news broadcasts.[4] If NPR wants more information or a different perspective, it may contact the social scientist who serves on its science advisory panel. If the story is about current anthropological fieldwork or practice, then it is a process story. NPR does some of these, and according to NPR's science editor Michael Skolar, anthropological stories that can generate interesting sounds are always of interest. Thinking about the live sounds in a neighborhood clinic, a bilingual classroom, a museum, or an archaeological field site should provide the anthropologist with a sense of what kind of ambience the NPR producer can capture on tape.

Long Stories

In much of the English-speaking industrial world, an emic distinction exists between "public" and "commercial" broadcasting. Anthropologists seem to think that public radio is the only place for dissemination of their work. The preceding discussion was meant to dispel this view. Anthropologists can and do use both public and commercial radio. Both kinds of radio have news, public affairs, interviews, and call-in programs. But for longer feature stories, especially process and "human interest" stories, public radio may be the most effective outlet, especially if the target audience is the English-speaking, well-educated, middle-class U.S. mainstream.

There are presently two major public broadcasting outlets for longer stories. These are National Public Radio in Washington, D.C., and American Public Radio in St. Paul, Minnesota. Both provide programming for local noncommercial broadcasters. National Public Radio's "Fresh Air" and "Talk of the Nation" are examples. There are other, smaller producers as well. These include independent production houses, like the one operated by Elisabet Perez Luna to produce her program "Crossroads," distributed by NPR. These programs have their own staff, offices, and time to consider longer radio stories.

In 1989, the Changing Relations Project's Garden City, Kansas, research team used cooperation among local producers and university and practicing anthropologists to generate two stories for national distribution by "Crossroads" (Stull et al. 1990; Stull, Broadway, and Erickson 1992). By working with a skilled local

The Anthropologist as Radio Producer

producer, I found that the local anthropologist can guide the collection of sound and narrative from local sources. Equipped with a high-quality cassette recorder and a professional microphone, the local public radio newswoman and I visited Vietnamese grocery stores and billiard halls to collect ambient sound. I talked a bit with the owners of the stores while she taped, and she sent the tape to the "Crossroads" producers.

Don Stull, an applied anthropologist at the University of Kansas, was then asked to tape an interview in the KU public radio station. His responses to a telephone interview by a radio producer located in Philadelphia were recorded with high-quality studio equipment in Lawrence; the questions were asked and recorded at a studio in Philadelphia, and the audio result was a conversation with good sound quality that seemed to have been done in one studio. This was then added to the ambient sound from Garden City and mixed into the final story. "Crossroads" found the story of ethnic diversity and accommodation in a small town in the Heartland to be interesting enough for national distribution. The collaboration among local and national producers, writers, and editors is a fruitful model for other anthropologists.

HOW RADIO WORKS: TECHNICAL QUALITY AND STYLE

National producers and distributors, and hence local producers, are fiendishly committed to high sound quality. No local producer with a hand-held recorder, a built-in microphone, and low-quality cassette tape will find success sending stories or features to national outlets. High sound quality means correct and close mike placement, high-quality recording equipment, and interviews conducted in the studio rather than in the field. Good content is the key to getting radio interest in the first place. Both technical quality and content have to be good, or your story will never be told on the air.

Using a Mike

One of my short radio pieces was once rejected simply because of mike placement. I had a set of taped interviews with elderly former residents of an abandoned Wyoming mining town, but I had been afraid to hand-hold the mike close enough to the speakers. The content was good, the equipment was the best available, and the loud ticking of the grandfather clock in the background of one of the interviews was mentioned as a strong point by the producer; but the sound quality was poor. The mike had been placed too far in front of the speaker, where I had hoped it would not intrude in the conversation. I was gently reminded by the NPR producer that a speaker cannot see a mike when it is correctly held by the interviewer—below the speaker's chin. My wariness to disturb the conversation with a hand-held mike prevented a tape from reaching a national audience.

To be an effective spokesperson for one's own work in an interview or a call-in program means losing one's mike shyness—for yourself or for people you might be recording. People do not like to hear their recorded voice for the first time. Because we are unaccustomed to hearing our voices without the buffering effects of our own cranial apparatus, we never think we *really* sound the way we sound on tape. Get used to it—that is, indeed, how you sound.

A program producer will try to position you close to a microphone. The closer you get, the "better" you sound, according to present-day radio notions of what "better" sounds like. But here is a problem. The miocrophone's diaphragm, which translates sound into electrical movement, responds violently to plosives and strong sibilants in human speech. The direct burst of air from a *p* or a *t* or even a well enunciated *s* may sound like an explosion if the mike is directly in the way of the air stream. This is called "popping the mike," and it is a sign of rank radio amateurism. Show that you are savvy by directing the stream of air away from the mike, while staying as close as you can.

Your host may provide a set of earphones (often called "cans" in some radio circles) for you to use. If she or he does not do so, ask for them. They will allow you to hear the studio or, on live broadcasts, the actual air signal that you are producing. When the mike is switched on, the room speaker always switches itself off, so that anyone without earphones has no idea when the music or recorded commercial ends and the live show is about to begin. The earphones also allow a speaker to listen to the effects of mike placement and provide a warning of possible "popping" problems.

When doing a talk radio call-in program, earphones are the only way to hear the caller without having the room's speakers feed back into the mike and cause the screech so common to public address systems at grade school assemblies. If the earphones are not shielded, that is, if they consist of foam padding without a hard shell cover, do not get them close to the mike. If you do, and the mike is "hot," or turned on, you may experience audio feedback in a painful and immediate way.

A Good Read

A "good" voice in news and public affairs means a clear and well-enunciated voice, not a particularly deep or musical voice. A good radio newsperson "can read." Knowing how to read is high radio praise. It means knowing how to read clearly, how to use the accents and inflections of English to convey the significance of text. Newspeople do not talk about NPR's Susan Stamberg's "great voice." They talk about her incisive questions, about her ability to *read*. While you are forgetting about the quality of your vice, it might also be wise to forget about your regional or national accent. It is an important part of your sound and makes for more interesting radio.

Radio Etiquette

Some points of radio etiquette seem to cut across all markets and all formats. Acknowledge that the producer controls the flow of the program, and if there is only one hand-held mike, keep your hands off—the producer will know how to place it. Recognize that "air time" is precious. Once an hour is gone, or a five-minute news slot is expended, it cannot be re-created. Parsimony is paramount. It is unfortunate that the 30-second sound bite has a bad name, because concise statements of complex research or applied work are genuinely difficult to construct and genuinely important if electronic media are to be used effectively. Have notes ready for your radio interview, but do not ever plan simply to read your remarks on live or nearly live radio. Be ready to ad lib. That means that digressions must be planned, and key phrases or ideas must be quickly, smoothly, and easily accessible to you on paper or in your head when you sit down at the mike.

Time—in the Western, lineal, and nonrepeating sense of the word—makes radio work. It is radio's key symbol and key metaphor. This means that when you telephone and want to visit with a program host or a news director, you must be attuned to the fact that he or she may soon be on the air. The radio programming "clock" is timed to the second, with news, music, or public affairs fitting tightly crafted slots. By listening, you may learn that the morning newsperson works until 10 A.M. Newspeople, in any market size, are under constant deadline pressure, often during several hours, to write or edit their newscasts. Plan your calls and your contacts right after the newsperson has been on the air, not before or during. Plan your meeting after the person's "shift" is over.

Finally, smoking in studios is not a good idea. Where station staff still do it, there is usually an audio engineer complaining to management about the smoke buildup on the electronic gear. Chewing gum and eating are not welcome either. A cup of coffee, however, is generally part of the ritual equipment of everyone working in radio (though public broadcasters are prone to include tea in their alkaloid repertoire).

An Intimate Style

Once the technical business of mike placement and headphones is taken care of, style begins to matter. In interviews or on talk radio, style with an interesting topic will garner a repeat invitation. The late Arthur Godfrey, long a network radio host, had much to teach broadcasters about style. Anthropologists wanting to use talk radio or willing to sit for extended interviews would do well to emulate him. Godfrey, so the folklore goes, would imagine his closest, dearest friend sitting across the "board" (control panel) from him. He would talk *to* his friend, not *at* his friend, using the intimate intonation and familiarity English reserves for close associates.

Radio is an intimate medium, even more so now that most listening is done in cars, rather than in family groups around the glowing mahogany Philco of 50 years ago. While on the air, do not imagine that 50,000 listeners are hanging onto every word. Imagine instead that there is a favorite student, a valued informant, or a close friend sitting with you. Do not say *they* when you talk about the audience. Say *you.* If you say, "They should come to the men's health clinic any time after 9 A.M.," the listener is distanced. Say instead, "You should try to come..." Use the intimacy of English (or whatever language you are using) to get your point across just as you would in a friendly, one-on-one conversation.

LISTENING TO RADIO

There are two major advantages to using radio for dissemination of anthropological findings and applied work. First, a radio documentary or news story is inexpensive to produce, and access to the results are relatively inexpensive (many communities in and outside the United States have easier access to radio than to television or film). Second, radio can target narrow market segments to help direct the dissemination of anthropological information to the intended audience. Talk radio offers a possible third advantage, by allowing listener comment and immediate feedback about the anthropological enterprise.

Using radio requires only a voice and at least one ear and the time and willingness to come to an understanding of the constraints and needs of local and national producers. Michael Skoler, who represents general science at NPR, says that the best advice he can offer an anthropologist trying to get material on the radio outlet is to listen, really listen, to what is being presented by the station or network. News stories that radio people find to be interesting will find an audience. Process stories with a definite, critical angle will always be welcome. Quality anthropological products, presented with a style and technique that are culturally consonant with radio's expectations, will always find a welcome ear. Anthropologists need only take time to listen.

NOTES

1. Frank C. Leonhardy, the archaeologist known for his Colombia River Basin chronology, was another anthropologist who financed

graduate training in anthropology with a part-time career in radio broadcasting. I always felt I could detect Frank's radio broadcasting experience whenever I attended one of his professional papers—Frank's prose was always crisp, to the point, and well enunciated.

2. This is something of a folk-sociological view that may or may not be reflected in the experience of most broadcasters: most radio broadcasters will tell you that to move up you have to move out.

3. The producer works for a major talk radio station in one of the top ten U.S. markets.

4. In addition to the long-standing morning ("Morning Edition") and evening ("All Things Considered") broadcasts, NPR provides hourly news summaries much like those found on commercial radio. Both the Canadian Broadcasting Corporation (CBC) and the British Broadcasting Corporation (BBC) offer both hourly and longer feature programming.

REFERENCES

Chambers, Erve. 1987. "Applied Anthropology in the Post-Vietnam Era: Anticipations and Ironies." *Annual Review of Anthropology* 16: 307-337.

Firesign Theater. 1971. "The Three Faces of Nick Danger" (audio recording). New York: Columbia Records.

Goldschmidt, Walter. 1988. "Applied Anthropology and Broadcasting." Paper presented at the annual meeting of the American Anthropological Association, Phoenix, AZ, November.

Goody, Jack. 1987. *The Interface Between the Written and the Oral.* Cambridge: Cambridge University Press.

Johnson, Norris Brock. 1984. "Sex, Color, and Rites of Passage in Ethnographic Research." *Human Organization* 43, no. 20: 108-119.

Stull, Donald D., Janet Benson, Michael Broadway, Art Campa, Mark Grey, and Ken C. Erickson. 1990. "Changing Relations: Newcomers and Established Residents in Garden City, Kansas." Final report to the Ford Foundation's Changing Relations Project. Institute for Public Policy and Business Research, University of Kansas. Report No. 172.

Stull, Donald D., Michael Broadway, and Ken C. Erickson. 1992. "The Price of a Good Steak." In *Structuring Diversity*, edited by Louise Lamphere. Chicago: University of Chicago Press.

Chapter 11

The Anthropologist as Media Anthropologist

Susan L. Allen

> [Our] general way of thinking of the totality, i.e. [our] general world view, is crucial for overall order of the human mind itself. If [we] think of the totality as constituted of independent fragments, then that is how [our] mind will tend to operate, but if [we] can include everything coherently and harmoniously in an overall whole that is undivided, unbroken, and without a border (for every border is a division or break) then [our] mind will tend to move in a similar way, and from this will flow an orderly action within the whole.
> —physicist David Bohm

People who can communicate through media channels are among the most powerful forces on the planet as we begin the twenty-first century. This includes journalists, commentators, broadcasters, writers, and individual "great communicators," ranging from Bill Moyers to Ross Perot to Madonna. The purpose of this chapter is to suggest that anthropologists—media anthropologists—can, and should, be included among this group.

Who except media communicators have the channels, the skills, and, thus, also the choice of "wiring us into the system," as futurist Alvin Toffler put it or of excluding some of us? American journalism long ago realized that the Marxist-Leninist slogan "Many ideas in a few heads and few ideas in many heads" defines an exclusionist decision-making model and that, to survive, a democracy "of the people" requires as many ideas in as many heads as possible. Because we are the fortunate children of these political skeptics, our populist brand of journalism, with its thousands of small presses and points of view, was created.

But journalists, reflecting (foreshadowing?) popular opionion, have presented a conspicuously narrow vision of "all" the people and an equally shortsighted view of the world in the past. Who are "all the people" in the final years of the 1990s, and how many points of view are enough?

Can our U.S. brand of democracy begin to incorporate more voices in its informed, decision-making community? Do we have the commitment to, and trust of, democracy that will be necessary if we are to build workable avenues for reaching citizens with the information they need for responsible participation?

Our forebears had no way of knowing that in the late twentieth century, "all the people" would suddenly come to mean the entire global citizenry or that a more holistic education would be needed to adapt ourselves and our institutions for the diversity that democratic freedoms make possible.

However, we do know it today, and that is why the late president John Kennedy predicted in the early 1960s that "our greatest challenge is to make the world safe for differences." If we really want an informed, participating population, those people whose job it is to inform us will need to expand their own perceptions of the audience, of the definition of news, of the notion of balanced coverage; and they will need to heighten their own awareness of culture and sensitivity to the need for global diversity, mutuality, and adaptability so they can share them with the rest of us. In short, our media informers will need to develop, and then share, a holistic perspective. Anthropologists and other professionals with access to the whole-world database and perspectives now needed by communicators will have to begin participating in this massive educational effort.

It is this background into which media anthropology steps, bringing together the long-established practices of journalism and perspectives of anthropology, helping us embrace the inevitability of a twenty-first century where "all the people" includes the entire population of the planet.

Journalists have never wanted to accept the role of "educators," because education too often has meant spoon-feeding popular dogma from this or that authority to an uncritical audience. But, as the world's need for perspective on itself emerges, such limited and limiting definitions of education also must grow to reflect the antithetical goal of liberating people from one-dimensional, myopic, and unquestioned views. Educators, including future media anthropologists, need to help us expand our critical abilities by using a more holistic and comparative database or, simply stated, by using and helping us build what Ernest Hemingway called a "crap detector." This is where anthropology, with its whole-world database and holistic perspective, can help.

Few (beyond those groups who support single-vision worldviews) would disagree that all people now need access to a frame of reference that will help us live in a global, as well as local, environment. We also know that to replace our fragmented images with more accurate, comparative images, we need exposure to information and insights that have the power to share those images. But where can we get "perspective-building" information outside the confines of the classroom?

I am not suggesting media anthropologists espouse any one, even new-and-improved, doctrine or narrow set of assumptions *through* the media; I suggest they combine the accessible channels and democratizing philosophy of U.S. journalism with an "anthropological" or "holistic" perspective to provide a more contextual frame of reference and critical grounding for conceptualizing all information. New media anthropologists can help accomplish this by adding anthropological perspectives through the selection of more diverse and broadly focused materials and, also, by reflecting larger contexts within the content of specific stories.

THEORETICAL BASIS

Media anthropology is a new field whose professionals, as we see in this volume, practice it variously. My own view is that the fundamental characteristic of media anthropology, which differentiates its "anthropologically oriented" information from good, in-depth journalism, is its basis in two fundamental aspects of anthropology theory.

The first tenet of media anthropological theory (and, also, of systems theory), as we have mentioned, is wholeness or holism. The old Cartesian, mechanistic worldview told us if we understood the parts of something (clock, body, universe), we could understand the whole. This framework has given us enormous, essential detail, but it has not been so good at showing us whence the detail came. Holism says all of the seemingly separate parts of a system are interconnected and interdependent; the whole is "greater than the sum of its parts"; and to understand any of it, you have to view it from the perspective of the whole. A system—whether an atom, a human body, a culture, or the entire global biosphere—functions as a result of the dynamically balanced interaction of all elements within it; no so-called part acts in isolation. So we need to consider both the parts and the whole.

Following the notion of wholeness comes the idea of relationship. This second principle of media anthropology, similar to relativism in anthropology, says all systems are composed of weblike connecting relationships: "If someone sneezes here, someone gets a cold there" and "What goes around comes around." Or, as the ecologists have shown us, "You can't do just one thing." To study and understand a system or to "cover" its seemingly separate stories as media anthropologists, we must be aware that there are perspective-yielding connections among individual elements and learn to see how they interact. Each element of the system has a unique, systemic individuality of its own (and most Western traditions would say an "individual worth"), and it also reflects and impacts upon other elements and the whole (a fact the Western traditions have largely overlooked).

This means elements within and among all news and information stories actually interact, even though they may seem unrelated, just as individual elements of a body or a culture connect, however invisibly or indirectly. Traditional journalism has focused on the seemingly independent stories, and traditional anthropology has focused on the seemingly independent cultures. This "fragmented" perspective is what we have been taught. For example, news reports are full of government officials telling us a particular event or problem has nothing to do with other events or problems. For instance, former secretary of state James Baker once said, "The Israel-Arab conflict has nothing to do with the Persian Gulf crisis." Politicians do not want us to think about interconnections because single issues are so much easier to manage. However, a trained media anthropologist would be able to say, "That's nonsense!" As the human body analogy has taught us, "parts" always impact on the whole. Let us find out how and then see if the relationship can yield important insights for the particular story.

An important task for media anthropologists is to help us realize that, regardless of how random the events of our lives may appear, actually all elements of our "story" and all "stories" fit into, and interact within, larger and larger systems. Journalists can no longer afford to reduce the definition of "balance" to the presentation of opposing viewpoints; we need to begin showing how events and ideas fit into a "balanced" global system.

ADDING A *W* FOR PERSPECTIVE

Even if we agree that media anthropology can provide a useful new form of communication in the coming information age, we still need practical and systematic ways to realize our vision. Metaphor banks and other culturally related cognitive frameworks always guide our thinking. Can we expand our mind-sets in such a way that we can begin to tear off our "cultural blinders" and become sensitized to the broadest possible perspectives? Can we find practical methods for teaching these new perception skills?

Who, what, when, where, and why—the five *W*'s—provide the traditional framework for newswriting. But the needs of our ever more visibly linked global environment have changed so in the past few decades that this original structure for "covering it" is suddenly one *W* too limited.

The original five questions continue to be the most efficient method ever devised for detailing the manifest content of a story, but, as I have previously noted, today detail is not the problem. Perspective is the problem.

Journalists "cover" enormous amounts of information, but

they are not trained to "uncover" the relationships and connections that exist within and among seemingly separate aspects of the information. The reason for this is clear. Our knowledge of the need to discern global connections is relatively new, and the old five-*W*'s structure simply lacks a question urging journalists to consider them. As a consequence, there is an urgent need—in journalism, in education, in private and public decision making—for a means of acquiring context and perspective.

Adding a *W* for the "whole system" to the familiar who-what-when-where-why reporting structure is one straightforward and systematic way to begin building a holistic perspective into the daily worldview presented to us by the mass media (Allen 1987). How would this new *W* work?

JOURNALISM'S HIERARCHICAL PYRAMIDS OF INFORMATION

Students of journalism are taught to structure their reporting questions through a framework called the "inverted pyramid." The pyramid is pictured upside down to illustrate that information is prioritized hierarchically, from top to bottom, as shown in Figure 11.1. If an editor needs to cut the story to make space for a big grocery store ad, this framework is supposed to assure us that the "important" information, the essential *W*'s, will have been covered.

This five-*W* framework can support all possible detail. But, as noted, without going into the "what makes news" debate, it is safe to say that what has been "essential" information in modern America has included little data designed to give us global or cultural perspectives or show us the interconnectedness of things.

The need for perspective is not limited to such stories as religious wars, medical research, or other so-called serious subjects. Take something as seemingly insignificant as a moment of dizziness. A "straight news" story from a 1993 newspaper might have said: "President Clinton [who] felt faint [what] as he jogged away from a McDonald's restaurant near the Capitol Hill [where] today [when]. It is suspected the president eats too much junk food [why]."

Figure 11.1
Journalism Inverted Pyramid

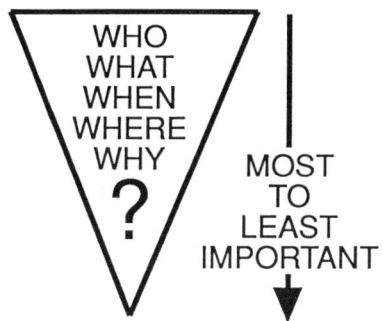

The five-*W* questions cover the story, just as they cover all stories. The "why" question even gives us some consequences and occasionally some context. But even the "why" question ignores that the president's light-headedness was connected to a whole body and a whole world that affect and are affected by it.

Another example: Americans learned in the early 1990s how little we knew about the people of the Persian Gulf region (and they of us). Our journalists (who, by the way, had told us practically nothing about that part of the world prior to adorning themselves with desert fatigues to "cover the crisis") told us Iraq's Saddam Hussein (who) attacked Kuwait (what) in the summer of 1990 (when). Iraq, they said, is a country somewhere in the Middle East where it is hot, where women wear veils, where men chant anti-American slogans and look like the Ayatollah Khomeini (where). Saddam attacked Kuwait because (1) the Iraqis were defending their heritage from oil imperialists (according to Hussein), or (2) the Iraqis were fanatics attempting to "steal America's way of life" (according to former president Bush) (why).

As mentioned, "balance" in American journalism continues to be defined as inclusion in a story of opposing points of view. Media anthropology asks us to broaden that definition to wonder, How does this seemingly separate event fit into the balanced system that is our world? In this way, we "add a *W*" for the whole system to the scenario. Who are these people?

What is the history of relationships that surround this particular episode? Where does all of this fit into the "big" picture? The goal is to provide, over time, as we can take it in, a "knowledge-general" framework that can help us better understand our world so we can outgrow our fragmented, fear-based, and crisis-oriented myopia.

Media anthropologists can bring to journalism the kinds of questions that acknowledge the unified systems that form the world; that signal our recognition that each seemingly separate story belongs within the context of ever larger stories; that make us more aware of culture as a blueprint for perception; that ask us to question any one fragmented point of view; that sensitize us to a holistic perspective (Allen 1987).

SUGGESTED STRUCTURAL FRAMEWORKS FOR "ADDING A *W*"

New media anthropologists can learn to think about perspective and more systematically "add a *W*" to their writing (for all media) with the aid of new frameworks that go beyond the elementary pyramid and the five-*W* structure.

Although they have not been emphasized by our educational institutions, including schools of journalism, some systematic relationship-finding methods already exist. More ways will be devised as we focus our attention on this pursuit.

For example, simply learning anthropologist George P. Murdock's list of the elements of culture and running mentally through its major categories can illuminate perspective-yielding slants on a story. Instead of unquestioningly accepting the surface-level explanation or prevailing authority's point of view, a media anthropologist interested in context would ask, How might this story [this revolution, this plane crash, this hospital bond issue] interconnect with some salient aspect of economics, politics, religion, kinship, language, local customs, and so on? As all mystery fans know, searching through the hidden connections and large patterns always yields unanticipated questions and answers.

For example, the "hidden" cause of a recent New York plane crash turned out to be miscommunication between a Spanish-

The Anthropologist as Media Anthropologist

speaking pilot and an English-speaking air traffic controller, in addition to the "obvious" explanation that the plane had empty fuel tanks. As another example, we are learning that a pattern of substance abuse links many seemingly unrelated kinds of "wrecks." Uncovering hidden connections and patterns can in time help us move beyond our crisis-oriented journalism and fragmented worldview.

There are also potential perspective-giving models that media anthropologists might adapt. For example, communications researchers at the East-West Center in Honolulu have derived a number of general themes that appear over and over in intercultural interaction (Brislin et al. 1985). In today's world "intercultural interaction" happens not just among travelers to exotic lands but in nearly every public school and neighborhood in America and many parts of the world. Adding an awareness of such themes to our media anthropology database can provide insight for many stories.

Good journalists have been applying important connection-making methods for a long time. J. Laurence Day, who was a United Press International (UPI) correspondent in Latin America for many years, told me that when a newsmaker came to the bureau to tip Day off about an event, he always asked himself, Why me? and Why now?

With the "why me?" question Day wondered how he himself might be an actor in the event. Did the newsmaker want the story leaked? Would Day lead someone to a source if he pursued the tip? Sometimes the journalist can be directly involved in the story; always the journalist impacts on it in some way because it is always filtered through his or her perceptions.

With the "why now?" question Day consciously placed the story, the fragment of life, the single pyramid, within the context of the past and future to check for connections there.

It is important to note that journalism, like all observation, is composed of a selective view based on some framing perspective and values. In other words, individual stories will vary from person to person, even when "the facts" seem "obvious."

If ten trained reporters cover a fire, ten different stories will emerge. One will emphasize the observations of the fire chief; one will focus on the contents of the building; one will point to the success of the "911" system. Because U.S. journalism cares about accuracy and because it has formalized the five-*W* reporting structure to give it uniformity, in fact all ten reporters will create a similar view of the fire and consensus reality for U.S. media audiences. (This is especially noticeable if compared with journalism styles in cultures where "objectivity" is not a particular goal.)

However, the fact that what we call "reality" is so dependent on individual perception is one reason training in the academic field of anthropology is essential to "doing" any form of media anthropology. As noted, anthropology is unique among all disciplines and other ways of seeing because it rests on an assumption of holism and relationship, and it has devised a set of cultural categories that is as close to a holistic database as we are likely to get. Even if no one can achieve a truly holistic frame of reference (just as no one can attain 100 percent objectivity), at the very least, training in anthropology assures us that media communicators will know that "adding a *W*" for the whole is an important goal. Certainly our news and information will never suffer from adding context based on anthropology's cultural categories.

VISUALS FOR PERSPECTIVE BUILDING

"Sunflower Web"

To help visualize how stories, people, events, ideas, happenings-of-the-world (all of those individual pyramids) may impact on one another and the whole, examine the extended pyramid model in Figure 11.2.

Traditional journalism stories stop at the base of single pyramids, just as their searchlights saw only one airplane in Karl Popper's sky (see Figure 2.1). They do not look for the connections that surround them in either space or time. "Adding a *W*" encourages us to transcend even an enormously detailed but one dimensional point of view and acknowledges the potentially relevant connections that surround it.

Figure 11.2 looks like a sunflower because its motion has been stopped. Actually, the model should look more like the sun

Figure 11.2
Adding a *W* for Perspective on the Whole

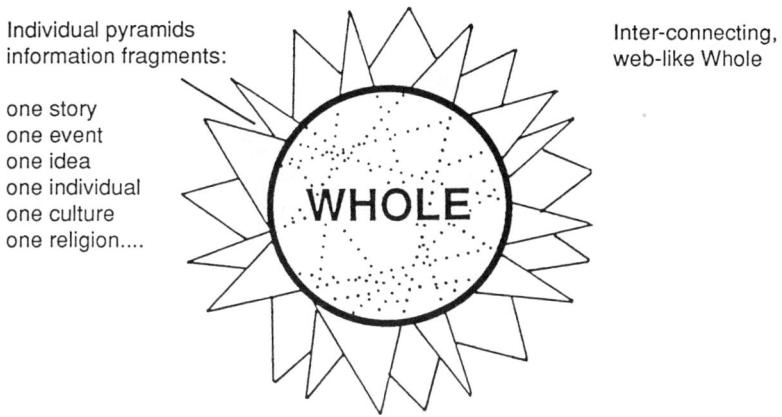

Individual pyramids information fragments:

one story
one event
one idea
one individual
one culture
one religion....

Inter-connecting, web-like Whole

itself: dynamic, asymmetrical, nonlinear, some flares (events, ideas) shooting up higher than others, some having more complexity than others. However, this model shows that all seemingly separate events in life make sense only when one acknowledges that they have connections and interrelationships.

"Hypertext"

A new and intriguing way to think about "adding a *W*" for the whole, or doing media anthropology in journalism, comes from computer "hypertext" theories (see Figure 11.3). Hypertext ("hypermedia" when various media are incorporated) is the sequential *plus* nonsequential writing/thinking that one can achieve electronically with computers (see Nelson 1987 for example). It is based on the idea that human brains know what they know not by thinking about individual facts or ideas in isolation but by making associations in an asymmetrical and flexible web of stored information. As with all metaphors, we know "this" by thinking how it relates to "that" and something over there.

The hypertext model is like the sunflower web model in its

Figure 11.3
Hypertex-like Model of How Elements Within Stories Might Connect and How Stories Themselves Might Connect

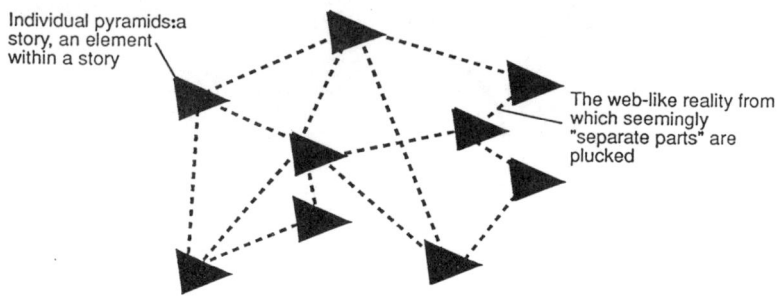

vision of numerous and varied levels of interacting information "behind" and surrounding elements or pyramids. Using hypertext within a computerized journalism story, one could select or highlight a specific word (concept, name, and so on) and, instead of ignoring the context "behind" the story, actually "click" supplementing information to the screen (and add it to the story, when appropriate).

A story about property rights on an Indian reservation, for example, might contain the word *mineral*. If the word *mineral* were selected, the reporter could "go behind" the superficial story and learn some of the history of the relationship between the government and the tribe concerning uranium. Another reporter might select the word *Navajo* to learn, and thus be able to add to the story, basic information about that particular tribe. A third might highlight the word *Arizona* even to see where the state is on a map.

Hypertext/hypermedia functions to program this more three-dimensional way of understanding information into our computers. Media anthropology asks for this questioning and sensitivity from our media communicators. Currently, journalism stories are presented in what is essentially a one-dimensional, linear manner. We even call it a "story line," as in Figure 11.4. Like hypertext, media anthropology seeks to add a more three-dimensional frame of reference to information, as in Figure 11.5.

Figure 11.4
Linear Story Line

Figure 11.5
Story Line with Associational Perspectives

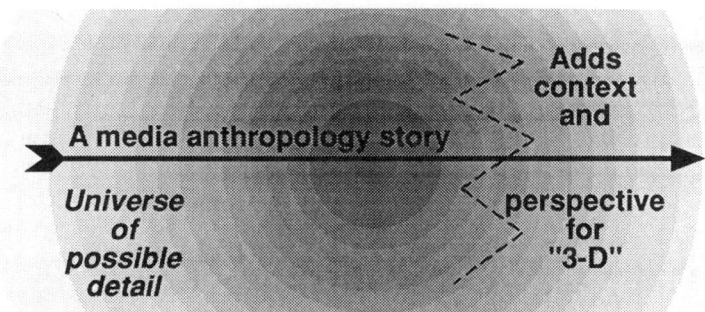

Working journalists may argue that applying perspective-building procedures would be prohibitively time- or space-consuming and costly. However, that is not necessarily true. It actually does not take long to become aware (1) that connections exist and (2) what some of them are. A sentence here or a new angle there is all it would take to "add a *W*" to most stories. If we are committed to moving beyond the one-dimensional story line and are trained to know how to add perspective, the question becomes, Which of the relationships can shed light on this particular story?

The question anthropology and journalism educators and practitioners need to answer at this moment in the history of their development is this: is perspective building an important new job for both journalism and anthropology? I suggest that it is, and that training is the key. Providing contextual information could become "second nature" for media anthropologists if they learn to think about information through perspective-building, web-like structures as opposed to hierarchical, story-line structures.

ANTHROPOLOGISTS AS MEDIA ANTHROPOLOGISTS

A true professional and theoretical synthesis of journalism and anthropology for the purpose of public education occurs when some of the new media anthropologists, with training in both communications specialties and anthropology, begin working in positions traditionally occupied by journalists.

For those coming to media anthropology from traditional anthropology, this will mean recognizing the value of the perspective that anthropology makes possible; realizing the critical need for an informed citizenry; and, then, learning to communicate beyond academe. For those coming to media anthropology from journalism, it will mean learning about holism, perspective, cultural and natural patterns, comparative methods, and other anthropological theories and methodologies—and then applying them to their work.

With awareness and with training in both areas, newly trained media anthropologists will be equipped to go beyond "covering" the surface-level detail of events and begin to "uncover" some of the patterns, themes, and interrelationships in which our lives are embedded and that give meaning to their detail. Where possible, in individual stories and also in the overall breadth of their work, knowledgeable and creative professionals may be able to generate insight that can, in the words of storyteller Kieran Egan (1986), "provide a tree to climb from which to view the entire forest." Or, in the language of anthropology, it can provide a "culture-general" (even universe-general) context within which one can begin to make sense out of the morass of "culture-specific" detail.

There is, of course, enormous, essential variety subsumed under any pattern, and the call to search for what Gregory Bateson (1980) called "patterns which connect" and provide common ground for our experience should not be interpreted as a mission to homogenize. On the contrary, it urges us to become sensitized to the diversity needed to sustain our dynamically balanced global system in the same way we name and value the seemingly independent "parts" of our organic body and in the same way we can appreciate both individual instruments and the entire orchestra.

Media anthropologists, trained to recognize aspects of culture and nature that can generate such a perspective and also systematically communicate it through the media, may be able to help others acquire this more integrated and honest way of seeing.

REFERENCES

Allen, Susan. 1987. "Adding a W: How Journalists Can Practice Media Anthropology." *Journalism Educator* 42, no. 2: 21-23.

Bateson, Gregory. 1980. *Mind and Nature*. New York: Dutton.

Brislin, Richard, Kenneth Cushner, Craig Cherry, Mahealani Yong. 1985. *Integrating Intercultural Interaction*. Beverly Hills, CA: Sage.

Egan, Kiernan. 1986. *Teaching as Storytelling*. Chicago: University of Chicago Press.

Nelson, Theodor Holm. 1987. *Literary Machines*. South Bend, IN: Theodor Holm Nelson.

Sogyal, Rinpoche. 1992. *The Tibetan Book of Living and Dying*. San Francisco: Harper San Francisco.

Postscript: A Cautionary Tale

Susan L. Allen

The career advice of my Vietnamese friend Tuan—Buddhist, economist, Bodhisattva—was to find work of service for which I have a "comparative advantage." When working in Washington, D.C., around the terminally left-brained (where I had no advantage at all besides being different), another friend, Mike, finished his law degree. I tried to strike this deal: if he would be my lawyer, I would be his anthropologist. It was a big joke even then. The absurdity of trading some need an anthropologist could meet for a job that could be accomplished by a lawyer was evident even to a naive young Ph.D. entering the labor market. After a dozen more years of searching for jobs as an anthropologist, I am reminding myself of my bird dog, Maggy, stalking the occupational thickets, almost out of instinct, anxious to point out my arguably serviceable but admittedly esoteric "advantages."

Although it is beginning to feel as though hunting may be my career, I still believe I possess a "comparatively" colorful feather or two some clever pointer might recognize as an "advantage," when spied among the other fowl in the bush. I have to hope my advantages (myself!) will prove useful in the long, wide view, even if no one is currently beating the bushes to employ them.

An ability to see life in holistic perspective seems to me to be a double-edged blessing for anthropologists: a positive blessing for many reasons and a compensatory blessing because, besides needing an anthropological perspective to do the work, it is critical for anthropologists to view their professional goals with the long, wide view, as well. When one's professional aim is to teach a universal perspective from which people can begin to "make the world safe for differences" and do it from jobs that do not exist and to people who do not want it, it is easy to see why a holistic perspective is the only salvation not just for an anthropologist's self-esteem but for even her mildest dream of professional actualization. They do not tell you these things in anthropology school.

However, this vocational woe of a misemployed anthropologist sounds more like the story of the "ugly duckling" than is probably the case. I am biased, and truth is more balanced. Traditional anthropologists are finding jobs out there, I am sure; it is just that my own 1990s reality has yet to top the 1960s dream.

In that regard, I might add that another pal, Dave, who is a minister, also admits to feeling daunted by the aims of his profession, but says there is always hope. He told me Jeremiah was so depressed about people's failing to shape up so he could reach his goals that he assured an entire population its city was going to disintegrate into a cloud of dust. Then, on the off- and hopeful chance things would turn around, he went back and bought real estate.

I am pretty certain I can be as optimistic as Jeremiah. So, in the off- and hopeful chance my comparative advantages may yet be of useful service to the world, I want to put on paper what I think some of them might be—for the record, as an investment in the future.

The kinds of things an employer buys when hiring an anthropologist are likely to include:

- a global, comparative, interconnected worldview
- a balanced, skeptical/critical/hopeful/holistic perspective
- an "anthropological perspective" that paradoxically supplies the structure for a nonanthropocentric, cosmological frame of reference where science, art, and spirituality can reemerge whole

Postscript: A Cautionary Tale

- an ability to offer comparisons and alternatives to most notions
- a familiarity with, and an appreciation of, many alternative cultural and disciplinary points of view, from academe as well as from experience through participant observation
- a physical, mental, and spiritual foundation tested by the alienation of culture shock and found to be surprisingly solid
- a sense of humor tested by bureaucracies both near and far and found to be thankfully resilient
- a positive history of working with different kinds of people, in a variety of environments—foreign and domestic—with a record of having fun
- a sincere and possibly even naive belief in equity, empowerment, the Bill of Rights; a belief that we are "in this together" and that there is no justice for one until there is justice for all
- a creative, nonconformist approach to most situations; an unapologetic antiorthodoxy
- a Peace Corps-style practicality and utilitarian approach to problem solving
- a long and varied relationship with the U.S. system of higher education (including insightful and unpopular books, some wise and eccentric teachers, and far too few students)
- responsibility; honesty; patience spiced with multilingual swear words
- a social and ecological consciousness
- a taste for sensible shoes, island light, appropriate technology, REI outfitters, and NPR
- justice as an overriding motivation for action
- a focus on individual worth within universal movement
- broad categories of appreciation for foods, friends, and customs

Anthropologists add to their advantages with an array of focused training in medicine, filmmaking, or archaeology, for example. My particular focus is "media anthropology," so it is fair to add some communications skills to the above list, as well.

For most anthropologists the job requirements are few: work that permits them to act on their values and a schedule that allows annual migrations to any place exotic; and, if possible: independence; a nonhierarchical, collaborative working environment; room for self-expression within occupational projects; a globally/ecologically based objective, at least in spirit; orientation toward something other than money—probably development, service, or education; and a boss who can appreciate being treated like whoever may be sitting at the front desk.

Bibliography

Allen, Susan L. "Predicting Reader Interest in Anthropology Column." *Journalism Quarterly* 52 (Spring 1975): 124-128.
_____. "Media Anthropology: Concept and Pacific Islands Case Study." Ph.D. diss., University of Kansas, Lawrence, KS, 1980.
_____. "Media Anthropology: Building a Public Perspective." *Anthropology Newsletter* 25 (November 1984): 6.
_____. "Adding a W: How Journalists Can Practice Media Anthropology." *Journalism Educator* 42, no. 2 (1987): 21-23.
_____. "Training in Media Anthropology." *Anthropology Newsletter* 30 (May 1989): 15.
Bateson, Gregory. *Mind and Nature*. New York: Dutton, 1980.
Bettelheim, Bruno. *The Uses of Enchantment*. New York: Vintage Books, 1977.
Bishop, Ralph. "Stones, Bones, and Margaret Mead: The Images of American Anthropology in the General Press, 1927-1983." *Anthropology Newsletter* 26 (April 1985): 18-19.
Bohm, David. *Wholeness and the Implications of Order*. London: Ark, 1988.
Brislin, Richard, Kenneth Cushner, Craig Cherry, and Mahealani Yong. *Integrating Intercultural Interaction*. Beverly Hills, CA: Sage, 1985.
Brown, Peter J., and Norman Yoffee. "Is Fission the Future of Anthropology?" Special Report, in *Ideas in Anthropology*. Santa Fe, NM: School of American Research, 1992.
Capra, Fritjof. *The Turning Point*. New York: Simon and Schuster, 1982.
Chambers, Erve. *Applied Anthropology*. Englewood Cliffs, NJ: Prentice-Hall, 1985.

_____. "Applied Anthropology in the Post-Vietnam Era: Anticipations and Ironies." *Annual Review of Anthropology* 16 (1987): 307-337.
Cherry, Colin. *World Communication: Threat or Promise?* Palo Alto, CA: Wiley-Interscience, 1971.
Coughlin, Ellen K. "Anthropologists Ask How They Wound Up in the Wings of Multiculturalism." *Chronicle of Higher Education* 39 (December 16, 1992): A8.
Egan, Kieran. *Teaching as Storytelling*. Chicago: University of Chicago Press, 1986,
Eiselein, E. B., and Martin Topper. "Media Anthropology." *Human Organization* 35 (June 1976): 111-220.
Firesign Theater. "The Three Faces of Nick Danger" (audio recording). New York: Columbia Records, 1971.
Fulbright, J. William. "The Legislator as Educator." *Foreign Affairs* 57 (1979): 719-732.
Galtung, John. "A New Order Is Not Enough," *Media Development* (April 1984): 1.
Goldschmidt, Walter. "Applied Anthropology and Broadcasting." Paper presented at the annual meeting of the American Anthropological Association, Phoenix, AZ, November 1988.
Goody, Jack. *The Interface Between the Written and the Oral*. Cambridge: Cambridge University Press, 1987.
Hachten, William A. *The World News Prism*. Ames: Iowa State University Press, 1981.
Harris, Marvin. *Cultural Anthropology*. 3d ed. New York: HarperCollins Publishing, Inc., 1991.
Haskins, Jack B. "Pre-testing Editorial Items and Ideas for Reader Interest," *Journalism Quarterly* 37 (Spring 1960): 224-230.
Hood, Stuart. *On Television*. 3d ed. London: Pluto, 1987.
Johnson, Norris Brock. "Sex, Color, and Rites of Passage in Ethnographic Research." *Human Organization* 43, no. 20 (1984): 108-119.
Jordan, Ann. "Commentary: Making Use of the Media." *Practicing Anthropology* 14, no. 4 (Fall 1992): 2.
Kottak, Conrad. *Prime-Time Society: An Anthropological Analysis of Television*. Belmont, CA: Wadsworth, 1990.
Lett, James. "Anthropology and Journalism." *Communicator* 40, no. 5 (1986): 33-35.
_____. "An Anthropological View of Television Journalism." *Human Organization* 46, no. 4 (1987a): 356-359.
_____. "An Anthropologist on the Anchor Desk." *Practicing Anthropology* 9, no. 1 (1987b): 2, 22.
_____. "Anthropology and Television." *Anthro-Journalism* 1 (October 1989).

McLuhan, Marshall. *The Gutenberg Galaxy.* Toronto: University of Toronto Press, 1962.

Nelson, Theodor Holm. *Literary Machines.* South Bend, IN: Theodor Holm Nelson, 1987.

Rosten, L. "A Disenchanted Look at the Audience." In *Radio and Television: Readings in the Mass Media,* Allen Kirshner and Linda Kirshner. New York: Odyssey Press, 1971.

Rystrom, Kenneth. *The Why, Who and How of the Editorial Page.* New York: Random House, 1983.

Smith, Huston. *Forgotten Truth: The Primordial Tradition.* New York: Harper & Row, 1976.

Stull, Donald D., Janet Benson, Michael Broadway, Art Campa, Mark Grey, and Ken C. Erickson. "Changing Relations: Newcomers and Established Residents in Garden City, Kansas." Final report to the Ford Foundation's Changing Relations Project. Lawrence: Institute for Public Policy and Business Research, University of Kansas, Report No. 172, 1990.

Stull, Donald D., Michael Broadway, and Ken C. Erickson. "The Price of a Good Steak." In *Structuring Diversity,* edited by Louise Lamphere. Chicago: University of Chicago Press, 1992.

Topper, Martin D. "Anthropology and the Mass Media or 'Why Is There A Margaret Mead, Daddy?'" *Council for Anthropology and Education Quarterly* (February 1976): 22-28.

Winokur, Jon. *The Portable Curmudgeon.* New York: New American Library, 1987.

Index

Abu-Lughod, Lila, 11
Academe: beyond, xviii-xxi, 1, 78, 133, 158; integrity, 6; job conflict, 119; media anthropology program, xxii; publishing, 68; review, 65; and television, 107, 111
Adaptation, 19-20, 23, 146
"Adding a W," xviii, 149-150
Agar, Michael H., 34, 43
Agents, 69-73
Allport, Gordon W., 1
Ambiguity, 20, 23
Ambrosino, Michael, 111, 114, 119
American Anthropological Association (AAA), 9-12; General Anthropology Division, 11; media anthropology, 2, 8; Media Workshop, 2-4, 8; public education, 13
American Anthropologist, 124
American Association for the Advancement of Science (AAAS), 8

American Federation of Television and Radio Artists (AFTRA), 87
American Public Radio, 138
Andropocentric, xviii
Anthro-Journalism, 4, 11
Anthropocentric, xviii, 19, 162
Anthropology: advocacy, 57, 86; attitude, 18; attitude about television, 91; humanistic anthropology, 29; message through television, 105; method and television, 85-86, 88-89, 93, 100; nonanthropologists, 31-32, 106-108; practicing anthropology, 29; traditional, 21, 24, 158; visual anthropology, 10, 29
Anthropology Newsletter, 9-12
Apadura, Arjun, 11
Asch, Timothy, 109, 124

Balance, 162; news, 24, 37, 151; in systems, 18-20, 148-149, 159
Bateson, Gregory, 8, 19, 25, 34, 159

Bateson, Mary Catherine, xix, 4, 9, 11-12
Beeman, William O., 9, 10, 12, 25
Benderly, Beryl Lieff, 34
Benedict, Ruth, 8, 25, 34
Bettelheim, Bruno, 21-22
Bird, Elizabeth S., 10
Bishop, Ralph J., 7, 10
Bluebond-Langer, Myra, 9
Boas, Franz, 7
Bohannon, Laura (a.k.a. Elenore Smith Bowen), 7, 8, 30
Books, 107; trade book writing, 68-79
British Broadcasting Corporation (BBC), 144
Broadcasting, 30, 92, 100; public vs. commercial, 138; radio, 131; television, 106. *See specific media corporations*
Brown, Joanna, 13

Campbell, Joseph, 7
Canadian Broadcasting Corporation (CBC), 144
Caughey, John L., 11
Center for Anthropology and Journalism, 4, 10, 11; Anthropology News Network (ANN), 12; *ANN Focus*, 12; awards, 11
Chambers, Erve, 10, 58
Cherry, Colin, 21
Chevez, Leo R., 9
Civil rights, 18
Close, Alexandra, 12
Collier, John, 10
Collins, Jane, 11
Communications: power of, 145; professions, 15, 18, 28; public, xx-xxi, 1, 4, 13; revolution, 21; skills and channels, 25; study of, 28; technologies, 20, 26; training, 25. *See also* General public; Media anthropology; Training
Comparison, as method, 19
Computers, 155
Council for the Advancement and Support of Education (CASE), 10
Crapanzano, Vincent, 10
Culture, 20, 61-62; awareness, 21, 31; beliefs, 17; blindness, 19; bound, 40; film, 106; general vs. specific, 158; knowledge, 26; patterns, 19, 158-159 (*see also* Patterns); perspective, 152; radio, 132; relativity, 38 (*see also* Relativism); sensitivity, 7
Curtis, Karen, 13

Dash, Leon, 39
Democracy: media anthropology, 146; participatory, 24
Dincolo, Diann McMahon, 12
Diversity, 19, 159; value of, 20
Dornfeld, Barry D., 12
Dorris, Michael, 11
DuBois, W.E.B., 7

East-West Center, 153
Ecology, xviii, 18, 128, 163
Eder, Richard, 10
Editorials, 47-59; op-ed, 48
Education, 21, 23, 163; information vacuum, 5, 24; journalism, 147; Mead, Margaret, 33; perspective-building, 30, 146, 158-159 (*see also* Holistic perspective; Perspective); public, xxii, 4, 20, 26, 31 (*see also* General public)
Einstein, Albert, 19

Index

Eiselein, E. B., 4, 5, 8, 9, 11, 27, 28, 92
Eisley, Loren, 7, 34
Elmendory, Mary Lindsay, 9
Equal rights, 18
Estroff, Sue E., 9
Ethnocentric, 19, 38, 56, 93
Ethnography, 38-40, 65; film, 106, 108, 126

Fairy tales, 22-23
Films: celebrities, 125; classroom vs. television, 108-109; ethnographic, 106, 108; making films, 105-130; reflexivity, 112; researcher, 125; scripts, 121
Flaherty, Robert, 110
Forward, Jean Susan, 11
Four-field intergrative model of anthropology, xxii, 89
Fuller, R. Buckminster, 19

Gardner, Robert, 109, 128n
Geertz, Clifford, 36
General public: AAA, 9, 13; audience, 2-7, 13, 25, 40, 78; citizens, 18; goal of media anthropology, 15, 21, 158-159; historical view, 7; radio, 133; television, 105, 107; trade vs. mass, 68. *See also* Global; Media anthropology; Popularization
Ginsburg, Faye D., 12
Givens, David B., 10
Global: anthropology, 18, 128; citizens, xviii, xx, 2, 20, 29, 146, 158 (*see also* General public); conscious, 21, 23; "global village," 19, 21, 35; issues, 26; journalism, xvii; worldview, 162. *See also* Worldview
Gluckman, Max, 129n

"Going Public," 12
Goldschmidt, Walter, 7, 8, 25, 131
Goodall, Jane, 7
Gordon, Tamar, 12
Gould, Stephen J., 7, 43
Granada Center for Visual Anthropology, The, 128
Granzberg, Gary, 12
Grindall, Bruce T., 10, 11

Hachten, William, 20
Hahn, Elizabeth P., 11
Hall, Edward T., 7, 8, 19
Harris, Marvin, xix, 8-10, 25, 30, 34
Haskins title method, 58
Henely, Paul, 128n
Hess, Fred, 13
Hillerman, Tony, 30
Holistic perspective, xviii, xx, 16-21, 93, 146-147, 161-164; context, 36, 44, 101, 109, 147, 154-159; human mind, 145; jobs, 6; public, 7 (*see also* General public); tenet of media anthropology, 148. *See also* Perspective
Human Organization, 4, 8, 10
Hurston, Zora Neale, 7
Hypertext, 155

Inclusive/Exclusive, 18
Interconnected and interdependent, 16, 20; news, 148, 155; way of seeing, 159
Interdisciplinary studies, 19, 163
Ivy, Marilyn, 11

James, Charlene, 4, 5, 8
Jobs, 6, 27, 29-32, 161-164; doing media anthropology, 157-158; income, 68, 102; newspapers,

62; royalties, 71-72; teaching vs. television, 119; television, 87, 91-103, 107, 126-127
Jones, Grant, 111
Jordan, Ann, 13
Journalism, xviii-xx, 10, 21, 23-25, 37, 40, 49, 63-65, 147-149, 158; culturally sensitive, 7; empiricism, 40; history, 146; interconnection models, 154-158; investigative, 39; media anthropology jobs, 30-32, 92, 103, 105 (*see also* Jobs; Training); perspective, xix, 5, 16, 31, 40 (*see also* Holistic perspective; Perspective); pyramid, 150-154. See also News; *specific media*
Journalism Quarterly, 3, 8

Kendall, Dave, 9, 10, 30
Kennedy, John F., 15, 146
Kertzer, David, 56
Kilpatrick, James J., 49, 51
Kluckhohn, Clyde, 8, 25, 34
Knudson, Ruthann, 9
Konner, Mel, 9, 34
Korbin, Jill E., 9
Kottak, Conrad, 12
Kramer, Jane, 9

Lansing, Steve, 113, 117
Lantz, Barbara Jo, 10
Leakey, Richard, 34, 45; family, 7
LeGuin, Ursula K., 30, 31
Lenz, Linda, 13
Leonhardy, Frank C., 143n
Leslie, Charles, 13
Lewis, Oscar, 34
Llewelyn-Davies, Melissa, 12, 128n

Low, Sam, 114
Lomax, Alan, 8
Luna, Elisabet Perez, 138
Lutz, Catherine, 11

McCrae, Stewart, 61
McDougall, Lorna, 13
McLuhan, Marshall, 7, 21
Magazines, 33-46; reader, 41; voice, 43
Marshall, John, 109-110, 124, 128-129n
Martz, Ron, 11
Mascia-Lees, Frances E., 12
Maybury-Lewis, David, 7
Mead, Margaret, xix, 7, 8, 25, 30, 34, 46, 86, 89, 112; Margaret Mead Award, 9; *Redbook* column, 3, 33
Media: and anthropology, 2; audience first, 41; internships, 8; mass, 25-27; orientation in work, 13; popular, 29 (*see also* Popularization). See also *specific media*
Media Anthropologist Newsletter, 1, 4, 8
Media Anthropology, xx-xxi, 5, 24; applied, 26, 29-32; characteristics of 162-163; doing media anthropology, 25, 145-159; early, 25; goal of, 26, 148, 162 (*see also* Education; General public); objectivity, 102; philosophical, 18; political, 23; psychological, 21; research, 26-29; systems view, 24, 156. See also Training
"Media Monitor," 10
Montagu, Ashley, 8, 34
Moyers, Bill, 7, 31
Myerhoff, Barbara, 113, 119

Index

Naipaul, V. S., 7, 30
National Association for the Practice of Anthropology (NAPA), 9, 11, 13
National Association of Editors and Broadcasters (NAEB), 8
National Education Association (NEA), 99
National Endowment for the Humanities (NEH), 111
National Geographic Society New Service, 3; magazine, 26
National Institute of Mental Health (NIMH), 3
National Public Radio (NPR), 31, 137-138, 140, 143-144
National Science Foundation (NSF), 3
National Writer's Union, 71
New journalism, 62-63
Newman, Kenneth, 12
New physics, 18
News, xx, 24, 28, 150; agenda, 30; balance, 149; media anthropology, 148; news peg, 49-50, 56; radio, 136; television, 92; and values, 55
Newspapers, 3, 28-30, 61-65; Associated Press, 30; columns, 58; editorial writing, 47-59; and ivory tower, 54
Nichter, Mark, 9

Oselig, Ruth, 10

Pacific News Service, 9
Painter, Andrew P., 12
Paleoanthropology, 19
Parades, J. A., 12
Participant observation, 101, 163; as method, 19, 28
Patterns, 19; in culture and news, 152-153; symbolic systems, 40. *See also* Culture
Perspective: anthropological, xviii, xix, 18, 36, 40, 61, 147, 162; cultural relativism, 127-128 (*see also* Relativism); emic and etic, 37; in news and information, 5, 24, 29-30, 56, 99, 149-159. *See also* Holistic perspective
Peterson, Mark, 11, 12
Pfeiffer, John E., 10
Pillsbury, Barbara, 10, 86
Popper, Karl, 16-18
Popularization, xv, 4, 25, 33-34, 46, 65, 106
Powdermaker, Hortense, 8
Practicing Anthropologists, 10
Practicing Anthropology, 13
Public Broadcasting System (PBS), 31, 111-113, 123, 130
Publicists, 76-79
Publishing, 67; editors, 73

Radio: and anthropology, 57, 131-144; markets, 132-137; sound quality, 139
Reductionistic, xviii, 16, 18
Reining, Conrad C., 2-5, 8
Relativism: cultural, 38, 61, 127-128; point of view, 19; and relationship in media anthropology, 148
Rhodes, Robin, 10
Ridington, William Robin, 10
Rodgers, Susan, 12
Roscoe, Will, 9
Rouch, Jean, 13
Ruby, Jay, 12, 112
Russell Sage Foundation, 8

Sagan, Carl, 16

Salvador, Marilyn, 10
Sapir, Edward, 7
Schuchat, Molly, 9, 11, 57
Schwartz, Douglas W., 13
Science writers, 2, 7
Scrimshaw, Susan, 9
Sharpe, Patricia, 12
Singer, Andre, 12, 128, 130
Skolar, Michael, 138, 143
Smith, Hubert, 112, 115, 121, 123, 129
Smithsonian Institution, 3, 6
Society for Applied Anthropology, 4, 12
Society for Media Anthropology: meeting, 11; organization session, 10
Society for Visual Anthropology, 10
"Spaceship earth," 19, 20
Stamberg, Susan, 141
Stepick, Alex, 9
Stories, 31, 110, 120, 125, 149, 153, 156-158
Sullivan, Nancy, 12

Tannen, Deborah, 9, 11
Tauxe, Caroline S., 12
Television: anthropologist as producer, 105-130; anthropologist as television journalist, 91-103; anthropologist as television subject, 81-89; cable, 26, 31, 127; "Cable Talk," 94-95, 99; collaboration, 118; film, 106; green room, 81-82; markets, 98; and media anthropology, 8-12; "Millennium," 12, 31; news, 92, 103 (*see also* Journalism; News); PBS, 31; sound bites, 85; "The Today Show," 81, 84-85, 88
Thomas, Lewis, 43

Tiger, Lionel, 8, 34
Toffler, Alvin, 145
Topper, Martin, 2, 4, 5, 7, 8, 9, 27, 92
Training: anthropological, 26, 56, 163-164; anthropological and television, 85-86, 93, 96, 100, 105-106; communications, 25-26; in media anthropology, xxi, 6, 11, 26, 29, 30; need for, 5, 26, 31, 154-159; writing, 45
Traube, Elizabeth, 11
Trevathan, Wenda, 9
Trillin, Calvin, 16, 21
Turnbull, Colin, 8
Turner, Terence, 12
Turton, David, 12, 128n

Universe, xx, 19, 163; human dilemmas, 23

Verdery, Katherine, 9
Vesperi, Maria, 9-11

Ward, Velma L., 12
Washington Association for Practicing Anthropologists, 5
Weiner, Annette B., xviii, 12
Wener-Gren Foundation, 8
Wilford, John Nobel, 11
Wilk, Richard, 12
Wolfe, Tom, 7, 62-63
Woodhead, Leslie, 12
Wordling, Daniel, 31
World, 16; shrinking technologies, 19; status quo, 19
Worldview: balanced, xviii, 18; culture, 17; filtered, 26, 28, 30, 64; soap opera, 16; Western scientific, 16

Yang, Mayfair Mei-Hui, 12

About the Contributors

IRA R. ABRAMS is a visual anthropologist, ethnographic filmmaker, and professional television producer. He is currently teaching at the University of Texas at Austin and producing anthropological projects for television.

SUSAN L. ALLEN is a practicing media anthropologist, currently completing an anthropology-based workbook on "valuing diversity," a textbook for journalists, and an academic curriculum for media anthropologists. She designed a doctorate in media anthropology at the University of Kansas when she became convinced that the way to get more media anthropologists on the job was to set a precedent for combining anthropology and journalism in an academic degree program. She did fieldwork on international news flow as a Research Intern at the East-West Center in 1977-1978. Allen has held a variety of positions in the communications field.

KEN C. ERICKSON is a practicing anthropologist and Bilingual Education/English to Speakers of Other Languages Specialist with the Kansas State Board of Education and a doctoral candidate in anthropology. His professional work includes refugee resettlement, ethnic relations in midwestern communities, and bridging language and cultural diversity in Kansas public schools. He has published on Vietnamese household organization, ethnic relations in social services, changing midwestern communities, bilingual education, and shop-floor ethnography in beef packing. Erickson has over 13 years of experience working as an anthropologist on the radio.

RANDOLPH FILLMORE is the Database Project Manager for AIDS Clinical Trials Research Organization in Tampa, Florida. He was the first Press Officer named by the American Anthropological Association and is founder of the Center for Anthropology and Journalism and the Anthropology News Network (ANN). Fillmore has supported his media anthropology habit as a free-lance op-ed writer, a food and wine writer, and a professional musician. He has taught courses in media anthropology.

HELEN FISHER is Research Associate in the Department of Anthropology at the American Museum of Natural History in New York City. She is the author of *Anatomy of Love* and *The Sex Contract*. She has been a regular guest on "The Today Show" and has appeared on "Good Morning America" and over 200 other television and radio talk shows.

JAMES LETT teaches at Indian River Community College. He has worked as a full-time television newscaster and is the author of *The Human Enterprise: A Critical Introduction to Anthropological Theory*. He has contributed articles to numerous books and periodicals including *Handbook of Religious Anthropology, The Hundredth Monkey and Other Paradigms of the Paranormal, World-Class Service, Current Anthropology,* and *The Skeptical Inquirer*.

CYNTHIA LOLLAR is senior communications officer for *Science* magazine and a free-lance writer. Her work has appeared in such publications as *New Jersey Monthly, The Atlanta Journal-Constitution,* and *Special Reports.*

THOMAS SHRODER is editor of *Tropic Magazine* at the *Miami Herald*. In his tenure, *Tropic* has won two Pulitzer Prizes. He has written features and special projects for the *Fort Myers News-*

Press, the *Tallahassee Democrat,* and the *Cincinnati Enquirer.* He was a National Endowment for the Humanities Fellow at the University of Michigan.

JACK WEATHERFORD is a writer and professor of anthropology at Macalester College in Saint Paul, Minnesota. He is the recipient of numerous awards including Fulbright, Marshall, and Kellogg fellowships. His books include *Tribes on the Hill, Porn Row, Indian Givers,* and *Native Roots.*